906

Hussein's Kingdom

915.695
2

28239

King Hussein and Princess Muna

Hussein's Kingdom

by

Winifred Carr

Foreword by

HM KING HUSSEIN OF JORDAN

 **LESLIE FREWIN : LONDON**

TO PETER

Contents

Author's Note

Spelling Arabic names in English is a headache. Whenever I have asked Jordanians how, they have always answered 'As you like'. There is no 'correct' way except to follow the pronunciation as closely as possible, and this is more difficult than it sounds since it varies from district to district. But I have tried to be consistent because different spellings of the same name, no matter how correct each one might be, are confusing and irritating.

I wish to acknowledge my grateful thanks to His Majesty King Hussein for so kindly agreeing to read my manuscript. I am particularly indebted to His Majesty's scholarship in the history of Jordan and his intimate knowledge of its geography.

I also wish to acknowledge the encouragement and help I have received in Jordan from Mr Ghaleb Barakat, Brigadier Ma'an Abu Nuwar, Mr Horatio Vester, my colleague, Mr John Halaby and my many other friends in the Holy Land.

For photographs, I would like to thank Mr Albert Flouty, Photographer to HM King Hussein, Mr Bill Beck and the *Daily Telegraph*, the Jordan Tourism Authority, UPI (UK) Ltd, and Syndication International.

For permission to reproduce extracts from *The Seven Pillars of Wisdom*, I would like to express my gratitude to the Executors of the T. E. Lawrence Estate and Jonathan Cape Limited, Publishers.

WINIFRED CARR

Foreword

by HM King Hussein

The Hashemite Kingdom of Jordan, The Holy Land, was the
first country in the world to attract those earliest of world travellers, the Christian pilgrims, who came to Jerusalem and Bethlehem. Centuries before this, it was the cradle of civilisation and a
crossroads for man and many cultures.

Today we have much to offer those from all over the world
who travel in search of unique religious and archæological
places, a varied and lovely landscape of fertile valleys, hills and
desert, a pleasant and healthy climate and a people who are
characterised by their sincerity, honesty, perseverance and
hospitality.

Our country is making tremendous strides in the field of economic development and, by 1970, the end of our current seven-
year plan, we are determined, with the help of God, to make the
Hashemite Kingdom of Jordan a self-supporting state, so that all
our people shall have a higher standard of life and that our
progress shall have covered every field.

Plans for agriculture, development and export of mineral
resources, industry (of which tourism plays an important part),
education, health, social welfare and internal communications,
and for developing the Red Sea port and new winter resort of
Aqaba with its unique seaside dry climate, are well on the way
to reaching their objectives.

But while striving to forge ourselves into a modern nation

as Arabs, we will never lose our inviolable tradition of true desert hospitality and for greeting as friends all who visit us. All who come to the Hashemite Kingdom of Jordan, the spiritual birthplace of mankind, are welcome.

The Coffee Game

LIKE ALL ARABS, the Jordanians are far more interested in people than abstract things and value friendship more than possessions. This is why they have such an unbounding curiosity about strangers – something you need to get used to if you are not going to feel constantly unnerved. For it is unnerving to be asked, quite unexpectedly, how old you are, then to be met with a long silence after telling the truth.

'How many sons have you?' usually comes next. Sons, you notice, hardly ever is it children. Among the older generation a man or a woman without sons is counted as being childless, no matter how many daughters there might be.

That hurdle over, the next question aimed at me is the trickiest of all. 'Miss Carr, why do you call yourself by that name when I have heard that you are married and that your real name is Mrs Frizell?' The first time, I carefully explained that a career woman (and that needed explaining too) keeps her maiden name for business purposes and that her husband did not get annoyed about this as long as no one made the mistake of calling *him* by the name his wife was using. Another long pause. Another silent weighing up. Then came the verdict: 'I understand perfectly, Miss Carr – you are a liberated woman!'

The next time I was asked this question I tried a flippant, but equally true answer. I was sitting in the gorgeously carpeted office of Ahmed Bey Loze, the then *Chef de Protocol* at the Basman Palace in Amman, waiting for an audience with His Majesty King Hussein, King of the Hashemite Kingdom of Jordan. So were half

11

a dozen Bedouin sheiks who up to now had been following my polite conversation with Ahmed Bey in deep, desert silence, their magnificent black eyes moving from one to the other of us like Wimbledon spectators, but their expressions giving nothing away. 'I call myself Miss Carr because few people can pronounce the name Frizell correctly,' I said. 'I am tired of being called Mrs Frizzle.'

'My name is Loze and people call me Lousy, but I don't care,' said this very important Palace official, and those silent, solemn sheiks, who of course had been following every word, practically fell about with laughing. It took a round of coffee from El Bishi, the King's personal Coffee Server, to quieten us down.

El Bishi himself was enough to freeze any first-time visitor to the Palace into respectful immobility. He stalked unsmiling into the room, nearer seven feet tall than six, old, dignified and impressive in his long black robe, a large brass coffee pot with a spout like a crescent moon in one hand, a nest of tiny cups not much bigger than egg cups in the other and a bunch of keys on his belt innocently tinkling against the silver scabbard of a wicked looking curved dagger. He had served Hussein's famous grandfather, the Emir Abdullah, the founder and first King of Jordan and had fought with him, the Emir Feisal and Lawrence against the Turks.

Later, when I knew the Palace officials better, I asked El Bishi how he made the bitter, black and spiced Bedouin coffee he always served to the King's guests. He took me down one of the Palace corridors and into his little coffee making room. On the shelf was a bag of freshly roasted dark brown Mocha coffee beans, and another of dried cardamom seeds. He showed me how he pounded the beans to a powder in a large brass mortar, made a strong infusion of them in a pot on a gas ring, then added a handful of the spicy, beige seeds to the boiling to give the characteristic flavour of real desert coffee.

Unlike the Turkish coffee served everywhere in Jordan and the Middle East, no sugar is added to the boiling to make it syrupy. The clear, bitter liquor is strained off the grounds through a bundle of twigs pushed into the spout of the coffee pot so that nothing is left behind in the cup when it is drunk, except perhaps the odd cardamom seed which has been allowed to float on the surface.

The cups themselves are without handles and the tiniest possible. They hold about a tablespoonful of the fragrant liquid which is meant to be slowly sipped and thoroughly savoured. The Coffee Server will hold a cluster of cups in the palm of his hand to fill them from the pot and, tiny as the cups are, they are never filled to the brim. This would be an implied insult – drink up and depart as soon as you can! It is the desert custom to serve the men first, then the women. This still happens occasionally in the towns, especially if there is an important man among the guests.

As soon as the cup is empty it should be held out for refilling if you want more. To take three cups of coffee is traditionally correct, but if you have not been told about the coffee game rules beforehand, your cup will go on being filled, as mine was to my shame, until you do as the others have done and give it a tiny shake of dismissal as you are handing it back.

With all the magnificent carelessness of a desert man at home in his tent, El Bishi would tip any dregs onto the priceless Palace carpets as if they were a stretch of sand, before collecting the cups into his huge palm and stalking back to his coffee kitchen.

Coffee serving is an important part of Arab hospitality, which is the most generous and graceful in the world, and bound by elaborate rules. Coffee is offered in most of the shops, especially the small, one-man-band ones, even though you might be spending very little. *Ahlan wa sahlan* – you are indeed welcome – they say the moment you go into anyone's office, and coffee is ordered, which must be drunk and enjoyed leisurely before starting to discuss business. It is a delightful revelation to anyone visiting Jordan for the first time, but a bit harassing if you are in a hurry to get something done against the clock, like catching the cable office before it closes for the day. You have to learn to accept this hospitable pause as graciously as it is given, and after a few days you will wonder why you could have been in such a hurry anyway.

On these occasions it is usually Turkish coffee that is drunk and a boy will be sent out to the nearest coffee shop to bring in a steaming, long-handled potful, specially sweetened to your taste. Your host will ask how you like your coffee, *helu* for very sweet, which means almost as much sugar as coffee goes into the pot, *mazbout* for medium or *murrah* if you do not want sugar. A pleasant tradition is that the sweeter the coffee the happier the occasion, but it is a difficult one for dieters.

Oddly enough, if you ask for tea instead, this ritual of sweetening to taste does not apply. Tea always arrives well sugared and is served in little glasses, without milk, and often with mint.

A Jordanian will always offer his guest the best he can afford even if it means going without himself, as it often does if he is a poor villager or Bedouin tribesman. There is an old Arab story, my favourite out of many, that illustrates this instinctive generosity perfectly.

There was once a wealthy prince who was so free with his hospitality that eventually he had given away everything he owned except his dearest possession, a beautiful white horse. The horse was famous throughout Arabia and the prince could have sold it for a fortune and become a rich man again, but although he was now desperately poor he refused to part with it. A neighbouring prince, knowing the situation, but also knowing that he would never be able to buy the horse, disguised himself as a poor traveller and arrived at the tents of the impoverished prince. Like any traveller in the desert he was received as an honoured guest and given food and drink without question. At the end of two days, the guest, as was the custom, was expected to leave, or to give a reason for his continued visit. He told his host that he had come to his tents to ask a boon. 'If it is my power, I shall give it,' said the host, and then the guest asked for the precious white horse. 'I have already given it to you,' was the reply. 'You have eaten it these past two days. It was the only meat I had to offer you.'

From Behind the Veil

THE LAST TIME I saw El Bishi, the King's Coffee Server, who was proud of his many sons and who must have been well over seventy, I congratulated him on the recent birth of another child. His glum answer was, 'It was a girl'.

Not that girls are despised nowadays, but sons are more prized than daughters and the men in Jordan really believe, as most men everywhere like to, that they are the salt of the earth. The word of the head male of the family is, on the face of it, law. Even married sons are expected to obey their fathers.

Traditionally a girl's father or her eldest brother, or failing them, her senior uncle, has absolute control over her until she is married. Then her husband takes over. But like many other traditions, this law of male domination is gradually breaking down and a strong-willed or clever woman has always been able to wield a power of her own.

It has become the custom among the men of the educated town and city Moslem families to have only one wife and this is strengthening a woman's position in society. Polygamy hardly fits into a modern way of life; in these days it is too expensive, since all a man's wives – and Islam allows him four – must be treated on an equal footing. It is a case of buy a gold bracelet for one and you have to buy one, two or three more just like it.

Women in Jordan have been promised, though not yet given, the vote. But through their responsible and active participation in social work they are managing to gain some influence in the Government. The educated women among the thousands of Pales-

15

tinian refugees who poured into the country from the sophisticated West Bank side of the River Jordan, during the Arab-Jewish
war in 1948-9, brought with them Western ideas of emancipation
which have had a great deal of influence on the more conservative
rural and desert dwelling families of the East Bank, formerly
Transjordan. The Royal Family of Jordan also give a lead in helping to emancipate women by setting an example in monogamy
and permitting the royal ladies to take a leading part in social
work. Queen Zein, the King's mother, is president of a society
which has fought to get reform in women's prison sentences and
has improved hospitals and medical services.

The King himself believes that women have an important part
to play in building up this new country, the Hashemite Kingdom
of Jordan, created in 1950 by the unification of the East and West
Banks. 'A lot of old conceptions are slowly disappearing to leave
way for modern ideas,' he has told me. 'There is now equality between boys and girls in education and women are playing an
important part in many social activities. The only thing we have
not yet reached is political rights for women, but this will come in
time. But I hope all this progress will come naturally, not by a
jump which might cause us to stumble.'

The royal ladies, including Princess Muna, the King's British-
born wife, do not wear the veil, but in public they always cover
their hair, as any devout and modest Moslem woman does. The
royal fashion is to wear a white silk gauze scarf becomingly wound
round the hair and throat.

Without realising why, I won the masculine approval of my
guide and interpreter, a corporal in the Jordan Tourist Police
Force, on one of my early visits to Jordan. 'You dress modestly, like
a good Arab woman,' he commented one morning. 'How's that?' I
asked him. 'You always cover your hair and your arms when you
go outside.' I hadn't the heart to tell him I was being more practical
than modest. The scarf was to keep the dust out of my hair and the
long sleeves to stop my arms from sun-burning.

Perhaps he was being old-fashioned by town standards, since
he was a Bedouin and had been brought up in the desert. But all

16

the same, women do run the risk of getting disapproving looks, particularly in the small villages and remote districts, if they go around bare-armed, just as they do in some of the Catholic countries around the Mediterranean.

You still see veiled women in Jordan, of course, particularly in the towns, and very attractive they can look if the veil is one of those fine black gauze ones that enhance rather than hide the face. But more townswomen go veiled today in out-of-date imitation of the upper classes – veiled seclusion used to be a status symbol – than because their families insist on it.

The Bedouin and the village women will sometimes pull her flowing head-shawl across her nose and mouth and turn away from a stranger, even a woman, but this is often because she is shy, not because she is used to being shut away in a harem and only allowed out heavily veiled. In the Bedouin tribes of Jordan women have never worn the veil and have always scorned the jealous attitude of the more sophisticated town families who insist on it for their daughters and wives.

Nowadays the daughters and young wives of many of the wealthier families, particularly in Amman, the capital, wear Western clothes and think nothing of flying into Beirut for a shopping spree in the elegant boutiques that sell the latest from London, Paris and Rome. In the last three years or so, the dress shops and beauty salons in Amman and Jerusalem have made valiant efforts to keep up with their fashionable young customers. On my last visit to Amman I was taken to a tea-time dress show, arranged for charity. The clothes, ranging from swimming suits and négligés to cocktail dresses, all supplied by local shops, followed the lastest trends from the top couturiers of Europe. I could not help but admire the up-to-date hairstyles of the audience too. Most of the young women have their hair cut short and scan the international fashion magazines for what is new. 'How do you manage to get the styles you want copied?' I asked a friend, thinking of the one and only good hairdresser I happened to know in Amman. 'Well, he was the only reliable one when you first started coming here, but there are about twenty of them now,' she said and passed on the name of the latest favourite.

Although even the well-to-do wives pride themselves on being excellent cooks – and it can take all day to make some of the more elaborate Arab dishes – they can still get enough servants to do everything for them. This leaves them with a lot of time on their hands which they usually spend, apart from their social work, in an endless round of visits to the houses of relatives and friends. They like to serve plates of fresh fruit in the garden on summer mornings, or if it is afternoon, a more elaborate offering of fresh lemonade, more fruit, home-made sweets, biscuits and cakes, and nuts and chocolates, finishing off with sweet Turkish coffee.

No wonder they do not keep their lovely young figures for long, but no one except the younger generation minds. Slimming is not a fashionable craze with them, and in any case, outside the sophisticated set it is still a sign that your husband can afford to feed you well.

At these little 'at-homes' the women will gossip about their world of clothes, children, other friends and relatives, the new house they might be having built in Jericho or Aqaba as a winter weekend retreat, and brag about their jewellery and particularly their carpets. They prize their carpets as Western women do their silver, and are connoisseur collectors.

Now that there is widespread schooling for girls, and women students at the new University in Amman, many girls are taking up careers as doctors, nurses, chemists, teachers, economists, receptionists and secretaries, but life within their own family circles is still very close-knit and hemmed in by customs which might seem harsh to Western women. At one time a man could insist on his right to marry his cousin. In many of the 'good families' they are still expected to, so that the girl will keep herself and her inheritance within the family circle and there can be no question of a socially unsuitable match!

Chaperoning is strict. Even an engaged girl must expect to be constantly tailed by her brothers or her aunts and mother when with her fiancé, but many of the young are managing to get around this one. Parents still expect to choose husbands and wives for their children, but they do not always have the final word. In an important family matter like a marriage, brothers and uncles must also be consulted and their wishes observed.

The girls I have talked to about this do not seem to resent what we would call family interference, but at the same time they are not accepting tradition blindly. They know what they are doing and think it is the right thing. 'If we lose our parents it would then be our brothers or our uncles who would be responsible for us until we married, so we must listen to their opinions and try to accept them,' more than one girl has said to me.

From time to time of course a girl will complain or even rebel against these restrictions and long to be 'emancipated'. But usually the more she learns about the emancipation of Western women the more she is horrified. To be nobody's responsibility, not even one's parents, after reaching a certain age; to be so much on an equal footing with one's husband that one can have a career and yet be expected to bring up a family and run a home at the same time, often without help, and worst of all, to be expected to pay a share of the bills into the bargain, is not at all their idea of emancipation.

A Bedouin woman on the other hand has always had more freedom than a woman living in a town or village. She can choose her own husband and accept or reject a proposal of marriage without being forced into a decision by her family. She can also leave her husband if she feels she is being ill-treated and will be taken back by her own family who will first try to reconcile the two, then pay back her dowry if she is determined to be divorced. It is considered shameful for a man to insist on keeping an unwilling wife.

As a married woman she can be hostess to men visitors to the family tent in the absence of her husband and take his place in providing the traditional hospitality of the desert. No wonder she feels the average village and townswoman still has a long way to go to catch up with her liberty.

In Jerusalem and Amman it is no longer unusual to see husbands and wives together at cocktail and dinner parties or eating out in restaurants. The traditional Arab way of men only turning

19

out in public is now thought to be old-fashioned. But women are still expected to have an escort unless they are going to a 'hen' party, and it is still only too easy for them to be disapproved of by the older women.

One girl who had graduated with honours from the American University in Beirut and was the first woman in her family – and it is a leading one – to take a full-time job, told me with amusement how she was gossiped about when she smoked her first cigarette in public, at a party, only three years ago. 'The word got back to my parents in less than an hour,' she said, 'but fortunately they are modern-minded. They just replied, "Well, she smokes at home with our approval so we see no reason why she shouldn't enjoy a cigarette at a party if she wants one".'

But not many girls would have got away with it.

Royal Wedding

THURSDAY, 25TH MAY, 1961, was the day that King Hussein, then twenty-five, married a twenty-year-old English girl who had been born in Ipswich, and until her engagement to the King had been known as Toni Avril Gardiner. Her father, Lieutenant-Colonel W P Gardiner, was attached to the British Military Mission in Jordan and Hussein met her for the first time at one of his own parties, a small, informal one he was giving for some young friends at his winter villa at Shuneh, near the Dead Sea.

Amman had been swarming with journalists – I was one of them – from all over the world ever since the engagement had been announced a month before. At 5.30 on the morning before the royal wedding day, the telephone in my hotel room rang, just as I was trying to get to sleep for the umpteenth time in spite of the lively comings and goings of the crowds of villagers and tribesmen and their wives, children, fathers, mothers, sisters, brothers, aunts, uncles and cousins who had been pouring into the capital from all over Jordan during the night. They were all wanting to make sure of a vantage pitch in the streets through which they were hoping the King and his bride would pass after the marriage ceremony.

Not even my London office could be ringing me at this time of the morning, but, just in case, I was prepared to complain bitterly when a voice, clearly not a Fleet Street one, said, 'Good morning, Miss Carr. I understand you still have some questions you would like to put to His Majesty and the Lady Muna. If you can type them out and bring them up to the Palace right away, I will see that you get your answers.'

Before I had time to ask who was calling, the caller rang off. It could have been a leg pull by one of my colleagues, but it was a waste of time going back to bed and trying to sleep, so I sat down at my typewriter and wrote out ten questions, including the one that everybody inside and outside Jordan was asking – what did His Majesty think was the general feeling in Jordan about his marriage to a non-Arab?

Half an hour later I had handed my questions over to one of the King's secretaries – the man who had telephoned – who had been waiting for them. The King had just come back from dawn prayers at the Husseini Mosque in the centre of the city for, as well as being the day before his wedding, it was the start of the great Moslem feast of Eid al Adha.

For the first time since I had arrived in Amman my taxi was not stopped and searched for firearms that morning as it went through the control post at the foot of the winding hill that leads up, through a garden, to the Basman Palace. This is the King's 'working' palace, where he has an office and holds audiences. Everybody was smiling happily and I was waved on with a shout of 'Good morning'.

In the courtyard outside the entrance to the Palace the Royal Pipers of the Jordanian Arab Army, dressed in white, their green bagpipes at the ready, were drawn up in line. The whole place, inside and out, was teeming with splendidly robed sheiks, their gossamer-fine brown abbas edged thickly with gold, religious leaders in spectacular headdresses, smartly pressed and polished high ranking officers and important looking Government and Palace officials and members of foreign missions in Jordan.

'His Majesty is with the Crown Prince at the Raghadan Palace receiving congratulations,' said the secretary. 'You can walk over and take a look if you like.'

The Raghadan is a fairy-tale palace with hand-carved ceilings painted blue, crimson and gold in classical Arab style. It is in the same grounds as the Basman and was built by Hussein's grandfather, the then Emir Abdullah, when he first came to Jordan and decided to make the small market town of Amman his capital. Although it is cool and airy, it is said that Emir Abdullah, a desert loving prince, used to prefer to spend the hot summer nights in his hand-woven hair tent which was pitched in the gardens behind the Palace. Inside the Palace, on the first floor, is the gold and crimson throne room, which is used for receiving ambassadors when they are presenting their credentials, and delegations of tribal chiefs who come to greet the King on national feast days, such as this one was. This was where Hussein and his eldest brother, Crown Prince Mohammed, were standing to acknowledge congratulations on the royal wedding and the start of the important Moslem feast.

A great heap of daggers and pistols was piling up at the entrance to the Palace as the well-wishers pulled them out of their belts to leave behind while they filed through the pink marble entrance hall, its fountain filled with flowers instead of water jets, and up one of the pair of crimson carpeted stairways to the throne room. As they came out they rummaged in the jewelled and silver heap to find their weapons and then stood around in groups, smiling and exchanging greetings, among the rose-filled gardens in the early morning sun.

Soon afterwards the King came out and walked across to the Basman Palace to shake more hands, this time with the members of the foreign missions in Jordan. His right arm must have been quite stiff by the end of that morning, especially since he had signed dozens of official notifications of his marriage to heads of foreign states the evening before and it was still swollen from a recent typhus injection which he had been given when he decided to visit Nablus in the north of Jordan, where some infection had been reported.

By the time I got back to my hotel, the Royal Pipers had started to play and the music, mostly lively Arab choruses, was pouring into the already noisy streets of the city from loudspeakers which had been set up to relay the King's speech to the nation.

In this message, Hussein had pledged that he and his future wife, in whom, he said, by the Will of God he had found the partner of his life, would dedicate themselves to the advancement of the people of Jordan.

23

The fact that he was marrying a British-born bride, even though she had now become a Moslem and taken the name of Muna al Hussein, a name chosen for her by the King and meaning Hussein's Wish, had caused many people inside and outside Jordan to fear for his safety. Many Jordanians, particularly the Palestinians dispossessed of lands and homes by the Arab-Jewish war thirteen years before, were still disillusioned about the role Great Britain had played at that time.

Some days before the wedding the King had been asked at a Press conference at the Basman Palace whether he had taken into account any possible danger that might result because of this marriage. He had answered, quietly and simply, 'I have never been afraid of anything. I have my belief in God, my belief in myself and my belief in my people. No matter what comes and what dangers I face, as long as I have these three beliefs, I am confident.'

Hussein had faced danger unflinchingly many times before, as we all knew. As a boy of sixteen he had been at the side of his beloved grandfather, King Abdullah, when he was assassinated while going to pray at the Aqsa Mosque in the precincts of the Dome of the Rock in Jerusalem. Since then he had overcome internal intrigue and murder plots against himself and all the time he had walked freely and unafraid among his people. At that Press conference we all sent up a silent prayer that tragedy would not stalk him again now that he had fallen in love with the daughter of a British Army officer.

'Some people have tried to suggest that I have forsaken my duties for personal reasons,' he went on to say to us. 'This is quite to the contrary. I believe in my duties and in my responsibilities and I also believe that they begin with myself. I have always been very lonely and have had to face many things and take many decisions on my own. My only nervousness about this marriage is because it is to a very great extent a completion of a part of my life that has always been missing and is one of the most important steps I have ever made.'

Neither the King nor his bride showed the slightest signs of apprehension on their wedding day. They disregarded military advice to fly by helicopter from the Queen Mother's Zahran Palace, where they were married, to the Basman Palace, where the reception was being held, and instead, drove through the streets across the city in an open car. Once again, Hussein's faith in his people and his sheer bravery had its reward. The crowds packing the streets clapped and shouted with tremendous enthusiasm as their car, flanked by the scarlet-coated and black-fur-hatted Royal Circassian guards, drove slowly by and police cordons broke as the crowds rushed forward, some of the people even managing to kiss the King's hand. There was a constant chant of 'Long Live Hussein' from townsmen and tribesmen thronging the roads, rooftops, windows, balconies, even the trees, and in relatively quiet spells we could hear military bands playing tunes like *Cock O' the North* and *Colonel Bogey,* and choruses singing the latest Jordanian songs dedicated to Muna al Hussein.

The King was dressed in a spanking white uniform, his bride in a lovely wedding gown of pale cream wild silk delicately hand-embroidered with tiny pearls and diamanté. It had been made for her in London by the top British couturier Ronald Paterson, in the record time for a royal wedding dress of ten days.

Muna al Hussein went to London to order the dress and buy her trousseau just before the engagement was announced and the royal romance was still a secret to all except the two families. She already had her engagement ring, an enormous square-cut diamond, but could not wear it in public since it would have attracted too much attention. Even when she went into Paterson's salon to order her dress, she had to be mysterious about it all, and could not tell the couturier for exactly what occasion it was wanted.

All that Paterson knew, to begin with, was that his shy and youthful client was mainly interested in having a wedding dress that would be easy to move in and without a train. After a while he realised he was obviously going to be designing a royal wedding gown, so he managed to convince her that a short, square train would add elegance and bearing and still not be in the way. Everything had to be done in a tremendous hurry, for the wedding was only a few weeks away. As it was, one of Paterson's staff had to go out to Jordan to make the final fitting and she stayed on to help the bride put on the dress before the wedding reception, for which it had been intended.

For the actual marriage ceremony, which took place at the Zahran Palace on Jebel Amman, on the outskirts of the city, Muna al Hussein wore a pale blue linen two-piece, a white silk gauze scarf over her hair, and no jewellery. It was a short and simple ceremony in which the bride and bridegroom sat in front of a low coffee table in one of the sitting rooms and were asked by a sheik of the Moslem Sharia Court whether they took one another as husband and wife. Both answered 'Yes' in Arabic and signed copies of the wedding document.

The bride was the only woman present. Her mother and Queen Zein, the Queen Mother, waited in an adjoining room with other female members of the royal family, as is Moslem tradition.

Lt-Col Gardiner was there to see his daughter married to the King, but as he is not a Moslem, he was not able to follow the usual custom and sign the wedding contract. This was signed by the bride and the bridegroom and the official witnesses were the King's brother, Prince Mohammed, and his uncle, Sherif Hussein bin Nasser, the Queen Mother's brother.

Immediately after the marriage everyone in the room shouted *mabruk* – congratulations – and the traditional wedding drink made from an infusion of rose petals was passed around in silver goblets, with gifts of mother-of-pearl boxes filled with sweets. Queen Zein gave a tea party for the women guests which the King and Muna attended and another was held in an adjoining room for the men.

We all knew the wedding ceremony had taken place when a royal salute of twenty-one shots was fired from the Palace. Not long afterwards the King and Muna, who had changed into her Paterson gown, came out and drove off through cheering, singing crowds, to the little white guest palace of Kasr el Diafeh – The Smiling Palace – in the grounds of the Basman Palace, for the family wedding reception and the start of their honeymoon.

I had almost forgotten about the questions I had taken up to the Basman Palace the day before for the King and Muna to answer, and by now I felt sure that they had too, and who could blame them? But I was wrong. A Palace official came running across the Queen Mother's lawns with an envelope addressed to me and inside were my answers, written by the King himself. A small, but significant indication that Hussein is a man of his word and will take trouble to fulfil a promise, even on his wedding day.

I had asked about their honeymoon plans and the answer was that it was going to be 'here at home' and perhaps later in the year they would have a short vacation in Europe and England (which they did have), 'but God willing, we will try to make of our life a continued honeymoon'.

In reply to my question about what he thought was the general feeling on his marriage to a non-Arab, the King wrote: 'That is not for us to answer, but we both feel that we have enjoyed understanding and support from the bigger family of Jordan.' Certainly, watching the joyous reaction of the crowds that day, this was true.

I had also asked a question on a matter which had caused widespread speculation and that was what title the bride would assume after her wedding. Until a few days before the marriage she had been referred to as the future Queen of Jordan but although the King's first wife, Dina, had taken the title of Queen, it was not to be. It seemed that the King of Jordan's consort, being a Moslem wife, has no official status and does not automatically become Queen.

The King himself has little time for royal titles and court pomp and more than once has said he is never happier than when he hears Jordanians call him 'our Hussein'. We knew this of course, but all the same we were surprised to learn, the day before the wedding, that Muna would not be known as Queen but as *Sahibet Essaoun Wallismah,* an Arabic title which even the Government spokesman who announced this news was baffled by when he tried to translate. 'The nearest I can get,' he told us, 'is Owner of Protection and Self Sovereignty.' And at our blank looks, he added

27

that he supposed it could also be taken, since Arabic is such an elastic language, as Her Gracious Ladyship.

All the same, I still wondered if the King would confer another title on his bride after their marriage, and had asked him whether in fact this would happen. His reply puzzled me a little until I heard the full story. 'Muna al Hussein as a name, a meaning and a title is what my wife wishes to have all through life', he wrote.

Later I discovered that two days before the wedding Muna had told the King that she did not want to be known as Queen since she knew he was happiest when his people called him 'our Hussein'.

'Do you think they will ever call me our Muna?' she said, and together they told the Prime Minister of her decision.

The King at Home

Y ET THE NEXT time I met Muna al Hussein she was a Princess.
The King had given his wife this title on the day their first child,
Prince Abdullah, was born. A telegram from the Palace in
Amman had invited me to go out to see the baby, who had been
made Crown Prince, and bring a photographer so that I could
get a series of features on the royal nursery for my newspaper.

Although wild anemones were making splashes of scarlet on the
brown hills around Amman, it was February and still chilly, so
the King and the Princess were living in the little guest house in
the grounds of the Basman Palace, in which they had spent their
honeymoon. In the white marble entrance hall was a vast cage full
of singing birds and, as I waited for the Princess in the gold carpeted reception room, a large and friendly Labrador loped in and
made himself comfortable on the deep cushions of one of the pale
gold brocade sofas.

Both the King and his wife are fond of animals. They had a
similar cage of singing birds in their farmhouse home at Hummar
about ten miles out of Amman, a small white stone house called
Dar el Alkair which in Arabic means The House of Happiness and
which had belonged to the King's grandfather. In the grounds
behind the Basman Palace there is a private zoo in which they
keep desert gazelles, now unfortunately becoming rare in Jordan,
and the lions given to the King by Emperor Haile Selassie of
Ethiopia. There is also a pet monkey called Rita which visitors
to the Palace often see being led around the gardens on a chain,
well out of reach of the rose beds.

The Princess told me that it had been planned that the baby

should be born in the Palace, but it was decided at the last minute that she should go into hospital. 'Although I felt very well, he was my first baby after all, and that's always an unknown quantity,' she said. She surprised everyone by leaving the hospital the day after the birth to return to the Palace. 'The baby was in another room and I couldn't see as much of him as I wanted. I also felt we were disrupting the work of the hospital because we had a constant stream of visitors. So I decided to take him home so that we could have him to ourselves.'

One of the little Prince's first visitors was his sister, Princess Alya, then six years old, the daughter of King Hussein's first marriage. Princess Alya and her aunt, Princess Basma, who is Hussein's sister and was then twelve, gave the baby Prince their own nursery collection of woolly dogs, a silver egg cup and spoon and rattle and an ivory teething ring. These gifts were displayed on shelves in the nursery which had been made on the first floor.

Almost everything in the room was blue, including the carpet and the miniature dresser and wardrobes that held the baby's layette. 'Most of the nursery furnishings were bought before he was born by one of his aunts who told us that blue was the only colour available,' said Princess Muna with a smile.

While the photographs were being taken, the King came into the nursery to say goodbye to his wife, but he stopped for a few minutes to pose for a photograph with the Princess and his son and it was very obvious that here was a truly happy and contented man. It was not long after this that someone who had been a bitter opponent of the marriage, for political reasons, said to me, 'I am all for it now. Princess Muna has made the King a calmer and happier man. She is a good wife and mother. The two things that matter most.' The following year another son, Prince Feisal, was born.

In the spring of 1965 when Crown Prince Abdullah was three, King Hussein decided to transfer the succession of the throne to his own younger brother, Prince Hassan, then eighteen years old and a student at Oxford. The news caused much wild speculation outside the Middle East where the Moslem tradition of a

leader nominating his successor and choosing the man he feels will
be best for the job, seems strange to those of us used to the rigid
tradition of father-to-son inheritance. Quite often it is a brother, a
grandson or even an uncle that is chosen.

King Hussein, who has no illusions about the constant danger
to his life and the political tension in the Middle East, was putting
his country first when he decided to take this step. He wanted to
make sure that there was someone strong, competent and ready
to take his place, should it be necessary. 'I don't fear death for
myself, but I do care what happens to my country afterwards. My
sons will be too young for years to take over and who knows how
small boys may turn out,' he said soon after announcing that he
had made his brother the new Crown Prince.

The first person with whom he discussed his thoughts was Princess Muna and it was planned that she should be with him when
he made the announcement. Unfortunately she was in London for
medical treatment when the news broke and her absence set
tongues wagging even more furiously. The reason for the mis-
timing was that a rumour of the King's intention had leaked out
of the Court and was beginning to spread in Jordan and the
Middle East. So the King had no alternative but to speak out at
once to put an end to uneasy speculation among his people. The
news was received with enthusiasm by the Jordanians who have
much regard for Prince Hassan and see in him many of the
qualities they admire in Hussein.

A few days after this, Princess Muna was back in Jordan and
she and the King were in the throes of planning to move into a
new house they had built at their farm at Hummar, on an adjoining hill to the one on which the old farmhouse stands. Their
old home had become too small for the family especially after
Princess Alya, who had been living with her grandmother, Queen
Zein, had come to live with them. More rooms were needed for her
and her two young brothers who were no longer babies, but active
little boys, and for the larger nursery staff. And there had not always been enough room for family guests to stay. So the King and
the Princess decided to plan a new, bigger home and use the

original farmhouse as an overflow for guests when they have an extra large house party.

It is a modern two-storied house designed to blend into the contours of the hilltop and built in local stone and marble. From the windows and the terraces there are fabulous views across the hundreds of fruit trees on the farm then the distant green hills, as far as Jerash and Jerusalem. The gardens have been land-scaped into the hillside with a lawn leading straight from the house where the children can play and eventually the King and Princess Muna plan to have a swimming pool and tennis courts added.

Pale beige Jordanian marble has been used for the floor of the living room which has a free-standing fireplace made from natural warm brown Jordanian stone. The two young Princes had to share a nursery in the old house, but now they each have their own room and a separate playroom lined with blackboard and climbing bars. The furniture is painted in bright colours and an enormous aerial balloon from which hangs a golden basket filled with toys – one of their favourite possessions in the old nursery – has been moved in.

Much of the furniture in the new house is teak in modern Scandinavian design except in the dining room where it is more formal and made in rosewood, and in the King's study, where it is upholstered in dark blue leather.

The farm is run on successful business lines and grows grapes, peaches, apricots and walnuts which are sent to the markets in Jordan and even exported to Kuwait. Both the King and Princess Muna are fond of horses and already their sons are riding in saddle baskets.

Stables in Spanish hacienda style are being built on the farm for King Hussein's stud of pure-bred Arab horses. Princess Muna has become one of the most knowledgeable breeders of this lovely and comparatively rare horse. 'I feel His Majesty should have his own stable of Arab horses, which he loves. They are very beautiful and there are not many of them, but since he hasn't much time to run a stable I have decided to help build one up,' Princess Muna

El Bishi, King Hussein's Personal Coffee Server

The King and Princess Muna driving triumphantly through the streets of Amman after their wedding in 1961

told me one day after she had been up until two o'clock in the morning to see one of the stable's first foals born.

The horses that had belonged to King Hussein's grandfather, King Abdullah, were the nucleus of the stud and the keystone was a magnificent stallion called Saameh, now a ripe old twenty-four years of age, that was presented to the late King by General Franco from the famous Ybarra ranch in Spain.

Another founder member is a rare *Kehila Akrusheh* mare called Gazella, a pure Arab breed, one of the oldest, that is almost extinct. The Master of the King's Stables, Mr Santiago Lopez, told me, 'She was being used to pull a plough when I first saw her and no one would believe at first what a wonderful discovery she was, least of all the farmer from whom I bought her.'

Princess Muna rides an Iraqi-Arab stallion called Jussou. The King usually rides his pure white Arab stallion, Cavalcade, or his eighteen-year-old mare, Jamila. Just before Christmas 1965, Jamila had a foal which the King and the Princess decided to call Tracer. It is a strange name for a horse, but Mr Lopez explained that it was born on the day that the King, while in his boat on the Red Sea at Aqaba, narrowly missed being shot by Israeli tracer bullets.

The bullets fell harmlessly into the sea alongside the boat. 'I was in the boat too and it wasn't very pleasant, but His Majesty never flinched,' Mr Lopez said. 'It might not have been intentional though, since the Israeli MTB's were using a towed target at which they were also firing.'

The royal stables also have two fine racing camels which are sometimes entered for the camel races in Amman and the stadium near the Dead Sea. At the end of the summer, they and the horses are taken down to their winter quarters in Shuneh, near the Dead Sea, a desert oasis that once belonged to Cleopatra, where now King Hussein and Princess Muna have a villa set in a lovely garden spilling over at Christmas time with hibiscus, Bougainvilia and the great crimson stars of poinsettia.

As well as riding, both the King and the Princess are expert water skiers and skin divers, enjoy desert hunting trips and both

C

like flying. Hussein taught his wife to fly his private Dove before they were married. But their favourite relaxation when they are in Amman is the one that really brought them together, karting.

The King is a founder member of the Amman Kart Club which meets on its own racing track at Amman airport once a month. There are two teams, 'A' team led by the King and 'B' team led by Princess Muna's father, Lt-Col Gardiner. The then Miss Gardiner used to go up to the Club with her parents to watch her father race and to help with the timings and one day the King asked her if she would like to drive round the track herself. Princess Muna soon became an expert and formed a ladies' team which, however, was short-lived. She now competes on equal terms with the men, usually finishing among the leaders. The King has become virtually unbeatable on the track and has led the Club to many victories in international karting competitions.

All the club members' karts are kept at the Club garages between races so that no one gets the unfair advantage of private practice. They are serviced by Jordanian Army mechanics under the supervision of Captain Maurice Rayner, the King's racing team-mate and manager of the Royal Palace garages. Captain Rayner used to be manager of the garage which looked after King Hussein's car when he was a schoolboy at Harrow and later a cadet at Sandhurst. Friendship grew between the two men and when Hussein returned to Jordan as King, he asked Maurice Rayner to go with him.

Every morning by ten o'clock, except when he is away from Amman, the King is at work behind his desk in his oak-panelled office in the Basman Palace. He frequently drives himself the ten miles into town from his farm and Friday is his only day off in an always busy week, the day he tries to keep for his family. Above his desk at the Palace is a magnificent glass chandelier, and on the wall behind his chair is a portrait in oils of his grandfather, King Abdullah. Two Circassians of the Royal Bodyguard stand outside his door, splendid looking, black-moustachioed men in uniforms of tall astrakhan hats, polished high boots, long, full-skirted coats in scarlet and silver-scabbarded swords. They are descendants of the Circassian Moslem refugees who settled in Jordan, mainly in and around Amman, after their homeland in the Caucasus had been conquered by the Russians nearly one hundred years ago.

The King's reputation as an international statesman increases with every one of the political 'summit' conferences he attends and older politicians who knew his grandfather well are beginning to compare him with King Abdullah.

During the past few years his duties and responsibilities have grown so strenuous that his medical advisers have asked him to take a complete holiday, if he can, every six months.

As well as being King, Hussein looks upon himself as a serving soldier, dedicated to the service of a nation which has an uneasy three hundred and fifty miles of armistice line with 'occupied territory', the country which no Jordanian will call 'Israel'. He is Supreme Commander of the Jordan Armed Forces, which includes the Jordanian Army, formerly the Arab Legion, the best fighting force of any of the Arab countries, which is mostly recruited from among the Bedouin tribes and, since the National Guard has been incorporated with it, from the men living in the frontier villages. The National Guard was originally formed to defend these villages from marauding attacks by Israeli troops.

The King spends a great deal of time with his Army but also moves around as much as he can among the ordinary people of Jordan, visiting the towns and villages, dealing on the spot with personal petitions and making sure that his office door at the Basman Palace is always open to his people. Sometimes his advisers feel he is trying to fit too much into his working day and personally taking on much that might be delegated. But King Hussein insists on keeping in close touch with everything that goes on in his kingdom, and although a modern minded man, in being as approachable to his people as his grandfather was, in the age-old tradition of the great desert sheiks. In the democracy of the Bedouins any tribesman has always felt that he has the right to appeal to his sheik and in this case, to his King. Hussein is not a man to deny them this.

The Golden City

Out of Palestine and the vast Arabian desert beyond it came the three great monotheistic religions of the world, Judaism, Christianity and Islam, and for many centuries Jerusalem has been a holy city and a place of pilgrimage for all three. Whether you go there as a pilgrim, a tourist or with a job to do when you arrive, as I always have, it is an emotional and impressive experience.

Somehow even the smallest incident seems to be charged with significance. You share a taxi with a young priest and a flashily dressed ex-cabaret dancer who is 'doing the Middle East' on a package tour, and you think of Christ and Mary Magdalene. You see a village woman riding into town on a donkey, her husband walking beside her, and you think of Mary and Joseph. You learn that you can drive from Jerusalem, through the Judean wilderness, down to Jericho, in half an hour, covering the ground it took Christ and His disciples a day or two to walk, and you take a second look at the map of the Holy Land and realise how small an area it was where the Gospel was first preached. But for the barbed wire and no man's land that make a bitter division across it you could easily circuit this area in one day, by car.

The plane into Jerusalem is always packed with travellers from all over the world, most of them making their journey of a lifetime and realising an ambition they have had for years. There is a confusion of languages, Greek, Italian, Spanish, German, French, English, Arabic and many others. Sitting beside you might be a Franciscan, a nun, a doctor attached to the United Nations Organisation who works among the refugees, an Arab housewife

36

who has been visiting relatives in Beirut or Cairo, an American millionaire on a world tour, a pilgrim.

If you fly into Jerusalem from Beirut at the time of the Haj, you might find yourself sharing the departure lounge with a group of pilgrims heading for another place. Moslem pilgrims from North Africa, Turkey and Iran, flying down to Jeddah in Saudi Arabia, before trekking the last forty-five miles across the desert to another holy city, Mecca. Many of them will make an even more picturesque crowd than yours, the women in flowing robes and veils, the men in elaborate headdresses.

From Beirut the plane takes off over the perpetually snow-capped mountains of Lebanon where the Pharaohs used to send trading parties to collect the precious cedar wood they needed for their temples, palaces, tombs and funeral barges. What was once a vast forest of mighty cedars has now dwindled to a few groves of carefully protected trees, but at least some are still there.

Beyond the mountains you cross a wide and fertile plain, the Beka – the Biblical Valley of Mizpah – in which stands the gigantic ruins of Roman Baalbek and in the distance is Syria's Mount Hermon, whose springs, once dedicated to Pan, are the beginnings of the River Jordan. Beyond the plain are barren-looking stretches of hilly land crossed with tracks and dotted here and there with dark clusters of Bedouin tents looking from the plane like currants in a slice of rich brown cake. In the centre, surrounded by gardens and orchards, is the great desert oasis city of Damascus.

Then comes the Jordan, a snaking, silver ribbon fringed with emerald green, that cuts through the brown and cream landscape in a series of giddily winding turns.

Should you fly into Jerusalem from Cairo, as the plane crosses the Red Sea you will see two brand new towns side by side at the narrow head of the Gulf of Aqaba. They look close and neighbourly, but one is Eilat on the Jewish side of the armistice line, the other is Aqaba, Jordan's only outlet to the sea. Somewhere behind them, hidden among the sandstone mountains, is Petra, the 'rose-red city, half as old as time'. A little further north is a vast stretch of blue, sparkling water edged by a range of mauve and brown hills. This is the Dead Sea and the hills are the Mountains of Moab.

The plane will make a brief stop at Amman, the capital of Jordan, the Rabboth Ammón of the Bible besieged by David during the battle in which Bathsheba's husband, Uriah the Hittite, died. The next stop, fifteen minutes on, will be Jerusalem, and you will be astonished to see that the city is really as golden as the hymn says.

Everything, old and new, has been built from the pure-white stone hewn out of the surrounding Judean hills which quickly turns to a rich honey colour. The great cupola of the Mosque of the Dome of the Rock above the place where Abraham prepared to sacrifice Isaac, Solomon built his Temple and Mohammed ascended to the Seven Heavens on his miraculous nocturnal journey, reflects the light from its gold-coloured metal cover and the gilded crescent that rides above it. In the bright sunshine the whole city glows like warm gold.

The trouble with Jerusalem, where history rustles evocatively in all the streets and every sacred spot seems strangely familiar, is that you will suffer a bad attack of mental indigestion if you cannot take your time about seeing it. There is so much to absorb that the emotional reaction you might expect while walking along the Via Dolorosa, standing beneath the ancient olive trees in the beautiful little Garden of Gethsemane or touching the rock in the Garden's Basilica of the Agony on which Christ prayed on the night of betrayal sometimes does not come until much later.

You might be shocked and distressed at finding holy places that seem shabby and full of tawdry, tasteless things. I have seen the dismay on a woman's face as she walked under the scaffolding of girders that have held together the entrance of the fourteen-hundred-years-old Church of the Holy Sepulchre since it was cracked by an earthquake in 1927. I have heard the horror in a whisper inside the vast, dark and dusty church that asked a companion to look at those awful artificial flowers around a diamond-encrusted gold ikon. And I have watched the disbelief of people hearing for the first time those hoary tales of petty squabbles between the different Christian sects for rights and privileges on holy ground. A new crop of stories inevitably has grown out of the events that went on behind the scenes during Pope Paul's visit to the Holy City in 1964.

First impressions are strongest, but what is tasteless to some can be wonderful to others less sophisticated; what seems to outsiders like a petty row over the placing of a lamp or the stretch of a curtain can be the result of a clash between deeply held convictions and centuries-old traditions of *status quo*, and it helps to remember these things.

Calvary is no longer a 'green hill outside the city walls'. It is in the heart of the Old City. The way to it is criss-crossed by ancient streets and alleyways and its summit is covered by the twin chapels of the Latin and Greek Orthodox Churches within the Church of the Holy Sepulchre.

Archaeologists now think that Golgotha was originally the site of an Iron Age quarry and that Calvary was a fifteen-feet-high pillar of unworkable stone which had been left standing by the masons as they quarried around it. They believe that over the centuries before the Crucifixion the quarried gaps around the pillar had gradually filled up with earth and debris until a little hill was made.

You have to climb a short flight of steps up this hill, just inside the main entrance to the church, to the two Chapels of Calvary. The altar on the left belongs to the Greek Orthodox Church and stands over a silver disc covering the place in the rock that was the site of the Crucifixion. Two discs in black marble on each side of the altar mark the place where the crosses of the thieves crucified with Christ stood.

This chapel and the adjoining one of the Latin Church, which is vaulted with blue, gold, crimson, black and white mosaic and contains paintings of the tenth and eleventh Stations of the Cross, are perhaps the most beautiful and calm areas inside the church at the moment. Scaffolding covers a great deal of the rest of the interior and everywhere there is a thick blanket of dust from the ancient stonework that is at last being rescued from the decay into

39

which much of it had been allowed to fall while the different sects argued their rights to repair and restore the building. After many years of wrangling and some damage as certain sects decided to go ahead on their own, regardless, the Jordan Government, which administers the shrines in dispute among the Christians, managed to get everyone to agree to start on repairs and partial restoration.

While this goes on, it is difficult to imagine the great church as it should be seen, and even more difficult to try to unravel the puzzle of which part of the walls, which pillars and which paving belong to the original fourth-century church built by St Helena, to the seventh-century restorations made by the Abbot Modestus, to the eleventh-century church built by the Emperor Constantine Mono-machus and to the twelfth-century building of the Crusaders which gives the church its present outline.

Puzzling as it is trying to trace the outlines of history inside the church, it is even more difficult outside.

On one visit to the church, with a friend who lives in Jerusalem and knows a great deal about the Old City, I was suddenly side-tracked into a pastry-cook's shop in the Via Dolorosa, at the foot of the flight of steps that leads up to the entrance to the Coptic Church. Not quite knowing what we were up to, I followed him through the shop and into the store room at the back, where behind the sacks of flour and nuts he pointed out an ancient wall, part of a stone gate post with pinion sockets in it and a stone pillar. 'This wall and the gate post were probably part of the entrance to Helena's Martyrium, the church which she had built over the place where she found the remains of the True Cross,' he said.

We walked back through the shop and up the flight of steps in the street outside to a terrace built above part of the Church of the Holy Sepulchre, and it was from this point that I could see that the building is not just one church, but a confusing cluster of many, built over the centuries. In the centre of the terrace a cupola rises out of the paving like the lid of a gigantic honeypot. This is the dome of the Armenian Church of St Helena, built over the original fourth-century Martyrium, and over which we were standing.

A smiling young monk, his complexion as black as his robes, greeted us. He was an Abyssinian, one of the priests belonging to the Ethiopian Church, who live in little cells around this terrace and who on the night before the Easter Sunday of the Eastern Church celebrate their ancient rite of Searching for the Body of Christ by circling the roof of the Church of the Holy Sepulchre while beating African drums and chanting in the ancient Ethiopian language. They are intensely proud of the fact that their Church is one of the oldest in Christianity and that their Emperor, Haile Selassie – the Lion of Judah – claims descent from Solomon and the Queen of Sheba.

Directly below this terrace is the place where the indefatigable Queen Helena, the mother of the Byzantine Emperor Constantine, directed the excavations that led to the finding of the remains of the Cross. The legend is that she tested the remains for authenticity by placing them beside a dying woman who miraculously recovered at once. The Grotto of the Finding of the Cross is a low cave in the southern apse of the Armenian Church which is within the Church of the Holy Sepulchre. The roughly hewn ceiling of the cave is black with the smoke of the millions of candles that have been lit there by pilgrims over the centuries. As you walk down the twenty-nine steps to the Armenian Church, which is hung with many beautiful brass lamps wrapped in plastic bags that are only taken off on high festival days when the lamps are lit, you can see hundreds of small crosses carved on the stone walls by Crusader soldiers to mark their pilgrimages, nearly a thousand years ago.

Many of the traditional Christian sites in the Holy Land have rival duplicates and even triplicates and the place of the Crucifixion and Burial of Christ is no exception. Most of the sites were discovered by St Helena on her mammoth pilgrimage to Palestine in the fourth century, but other discoveries continue to be made.

The Garden Tomb is a new rival to the great Church of the Holy Sepulchre for the site of Christ's burial. This Tomb, which was discovered at the beginning of this century, is carved out of a rocky hill which rises just outside the present city walls to the

41

north of the Damascus Gate. The crest of the hill is an ancient cemetery and the side that butts on to the street is a car park. But the side in which the Tomb was found is peculiarly holed with caves and ridges that roughly suggest the face of a skull, especially in the bewitching light of early evening.

General Gordon, who was, like many soldiers in the Middle East have been, a keen archaeologist and a deeply religious man, became convinced in 1883 that this hill was Golgotha, 'the place of a skull'; that the Crucifixion must have taken place on its summit and that if the hill were excavated, the Holy Sepulchre would be found. He had to go off to Khartoum before he could complete his digging, but others carried on and found not only a tomb but the site of an ancient garden with a cistern and wine press. Could this have been the tomb and the garden of Joseph of Arimathaea described in the Gospel of St John?

Certainly it looks much more as one would expect after reading the Gospel. But it has not had sixteen hundred years of riches in architecture, gold, silver, precious stones and marble added to it by the devout. The ancient garden has been restored and now the Tomb's setting is shaded by trees and fragrant with lavender, rosemary, sweet smelling herbs and flowers. Whatever you might feel about its brave challenge to the mighty church at the top of the Via Dolorosa, it is a peaceful spot and satisfies the emotional need of many pilgrims.

One evening, as the light was beginning to fade, I was standing just inside the city wall near the Damascus Gate, on the roof of the Spafford Hospital for Children with Mr Horatio Vester, the son of the founder, trying to snatch a last photograph of the fascinating roof tops of Jerusalem. 'It was on this roof that General Gordon used to sit in the evenings, contemplating Jerusalem and gradually getting the idea that it was built in the shape of a human body,' said Mr Vester. 'In those days the hospital was the home of my grandparents, Mr and Mrs Horatio G Spafford, who left America in the 1880s to live in Jerusalem. The General was a great friend of theirs. As this idea of his grew he decided that the little hill you can see over there must be Golgotha because it is in the place where the head would be of the mystical body that he thought was Jerusalem.'

Mr Vester pointed over towards the Garden Tomb and the hill that is now called Gordon's Calvary, and it is true that from this rooftop it seems to have a skull-like outline, especially if you are looking for one.

The Spaffords were one of the first American families to make their home in Jerusalem. A few years after Gordon left they turned their house into a school of handicraft and dressmaking and eventually it became a children's home and hospital. It still is the only one dealing exclusively with children in the city and is run as a charity by their daughter, Mrs Bertha Spafford Vester. Her daughter, Mrs Frieda Vester Ward, is matron and there is a resident staff of nurses and doctors, including an orthopaedic specialist, since many of the children have to be treated for malformation of the limbs caused by diet deficiencies. There is also a well equipped operating theatre and a post-natal clinic where mothers are taught how to care for their newly born babies. The hospital can take fifty-five children and somehow manages to run on a cost of just less than £215 a year for each bed. This must be the lowest running cost of any modern hospital in the world and is an example of what wonders inspired hard work can achieve.

The children of Jerusalem are a delight. Bonny and friendly, even though some of them – the children of refugees – might be without shoes and wearing somebody else's reach-me-downs, they have a dignity that is unique in the Middle East. Of course, out of school hours some hang around the tourist spots as children will anywhere, hoping to make a little baksheesh. But they have to be smart to dodge the watchful Tourist Police, and they never make a nuisance of themselves.

Salah was one I grew very fond of; a small, dark-haired boy of six with enormous brown eyes, an endearing gap in his front teeth and a hefty pair of braces holding up his purple corduroy pants. He found me outside the Church of the Holy Sepulchre one afternoon when I was trying to decide which street to take to the Dome of the Rock. He knew I was lost, but he did not speak at first. He

43

just followed me and every time I stopped to look at the street map, there he was, dying for me to ask him the way, but not wanting to be the first to say anything. He won. I asked him if he knew how to get to the Mosque. Not only did he know but, for such a tiny boy, he also spoke remarkably good English, which he said he was learning at school.

By the time we had reached the Dome of the Rock, Salah had collected a bunch of chums and rivals who filed along behind me through the narrow streets as though I were the Pied Piper. According to their standing, they were greeted with a smile or a scowl by Salah and every now and then we all stopped while they argued which was the best short cut to take. A large Tourist Policeman eventually broke the party up and they scampered off home like a flock of pigeons. But I bumped into Salah, still in his distinctive purple pants, all over the city for days, and together we must have walked for miles.

Apart from the many Christian holy places which are in the Old City of Jerusalem only two, David's Tomb and the site of the Last Supper, are on the Israeli side. You will be welcomed inside the second holiest place in the Moslem world, the beautiful Mosque of the Dome of the Rock. Mosques in Jordan are not forbidden ground to all but Moslems as they are in some Arab countries. This one, built on Mount Moriah by the Omayyad Caliph Abd Al Malik, between 685 and 691 AD is the earliest example of Islamic architecture surviving today, and one of the loveliest monuments in the world. Smaller domes, minarets and fountains surround it in the great marble courtyard of the *Al-Haram Esh-Sharif* – the Noble Sanctuary – and it is impressively approached from all sides by wide flights of steps and through graceful marble arches.

The layers of history that are concentrated in this place are formidable. Abraham prepared to sacrifice his son Isaac here and later it was the site of the threshing floor which David bought from Oman the Jebusite so that he could build an altar on it, over which his son Solomon erected a magnificent temple. This was destroyed by Nebuchadnezzar when the Jews were taken to Babylon in captivity. The temple was later rebuilt by Zorobabel and then by Herod the Great, and it was Herod's Temple that Christ knew. In 70 AD, during the Roman sacking of Jerusalem, the Temple was finally destroyed and, sixty-five years later in an attempt to obliterate even its memory, the Roman Emperor Hadrian built a temple dedicated to Jupiter Capitolinus on the site.

This temple in its turn was blotted out. The destroyer was Queen Helena, who was as industrious in demolishing the Holy Land's pagan shrines as she was in discovering the Christian ones. After Helena's desolation of Mount Moriah, it gradually became Jerusalem's rubbish dump until the arrival of Islam when the Prophet Mohammed made it the first Qiblah – the place towards which Moslems pray. The Prophet later changed the Qiblah to the Ka'abah in Mecca but to the Moslems Mount Moriah is still a holy place. When the first of the Moslem Caliphs, Omar Ibn Al Khattab, entered Jerusalem in 638 AD he personally helped to clear the rubbish that had accumulated on Mount Moriah since Helena's time, and ordered a simple wooden mosque to be built on the site.

The whole Sanctuary area, which covers about thirty-four acres, is protected by walls. On the eastern side, the wall is also part of the great wall of the city and contains the Golden Gate, through which Christ is said to have entered Jerusalem on Palm Sunday, and which has been completely blocked since the beginning of the sixteenth century. The gate was walled in by the Turks because of a tradition that the Christians would recapture the city by entering through this gate.

On the base of the southern side of the western wall is the Wailing Wall built of enormous blocks of stone, all that is left of Herod's Temple. This is where the Jews used to collect to pray and lament over the final destruction of the Temple by the Romans in 70 AD. This is also revered by the Moslems as being where the Prophet Mohammed left Al Buraq, the winged horse that carried him on his miraculous night journey from Mecca.

At one time, the great Dome was covered with gold leaf that used to be protected in winter with an enormous 'tea cosy' made from sables and presented to the Mosque by a Russian Czar. But the sables and the gold leaf have long since disappeared and the roof is now covered by a modern metal alloy that glints like gold, but is more protective.

The outside of the Mosque is covered with marble and hand-painted faience tiles and the topmost row is inscribed with verses from the Koran written in flowing arabesque letters of white on blue. Felt overshoes are provided at the entrance so that the priceless Persian carpets that cover the marble floor will not be spoilt. The building is impressive enough from the outside, but inside it is a rich feast of colourful mosaics, gilding, mother-of-pearl inlay, delicate carving, veined marble and wonderful stained glass. It is the original model for many Christian churches in Europe, Temple Church in London and Aix-la-Chapelle in Paris being the two most famous, for the Crusaders, who greatly admired its beauty, carried the memory of it home with them.

The Crusaders also turned it into a Christian church during their occupation of Jerusalem in the twelfth century (from June 1099), built an altar on the sacred rock of Abraham's intended sacrifice, fastened a gold- and diamond-studded image of Christ on to one of the doors, and a golden Cross on the cupola. They could not resist breaking off lumps of the rock to take home as souvenirs, and later the priests built up a thriving revenue for the church by selling pieces for their weight in gold, to pilgrims. Eventually the Crusader Kings of Jerusalem, afraid the rock would gradually disappear, put an end to this, covered it with marble and fenced it off with a beautifully worked iron grill that is now in the museum in the Temple area.

Breathtakingly lovely as the Mosque is, the thing that impressed me most was not the contrast in beauty to our own holiest of places, the Church of the Holy Sepulchre, but the contrast in atmosphere. This place of worship is lovingly cared for and peacefully free from wranglings over *status quo* by differing sects.

The earthquakes in 1927 and 1936 that shook the foundations of the Church of the Holy Sepulchre also caused considerable damage to the Mosque. Then damp from the faulty drainage system around the cupola loosened many tiles and helped to weaken the structure of the Dome. Some of the Moslem states contributed to repairs and restoration, which are now complete and a gift was made of £60,000's worth of handpainted tiles to replace those broken. In the nineteen-twenties a family of faience workers were brought from Turkey to make new tiles for the Mosque and to supervise their placing. Descendants of the family are still there and have turned their workshop into the Palestine Pottery where they now make inexpensive and beautiful things ranging from tiles handpainted with traditional patterns of stylised flowers, birds, gazelles and arabesque designs such as you see in oriental carpets, to plates, beer mugs, tea and coffee sets and doorknobs. Visitors to the pottery can watch the potters at the wheels, see the damp clay shapes being stacked into the kiln for baking and choose their own combination of designs and colours for the artists to paint on before the final glazing.

Every window in the many goldsmiths' shops in Jerusalem is crammed with bracelets, bangles, rings, necklaces, earrings and other baubles worth a sheik's ransom at home prices, but here untaxed and therefore cheaper than jewellery I have found anywhere else. Diamonds may be a girl's best friend, but not in Jordan. It is gold. An old-fashioned Arab husband, particularly a Bedouin, will convert his wife's marriage dowry into as many heavy gold bracelets her wrists and her father's pocket can bear. This gold then becomes her personal bank account for a rainy day.

Buying it is a fascinating business. Coffee is sent for and chairs are pulled up to the counter while the goldsmith weighs everything on tiny brass scales to calculate the price. Arab gold is usually eighteen or twenty carat and sold by the gramme with little regard for the cost of often exquisite workmanship. If a ring does not fit, the goldsmith using a graduated steel tube and a wooden mallet will 'stretch' it. If a necklace chain is too long, he will shorten it on the spot. If you like a bracelet but prefer it set with different coloured stones, choose the stones you want from a baize-lined tray and they will be set for you by the time you come back the next morning.

47

Such leisurely shopping can lead to friendships as you get talking to the shopkeepers. The happiest afternoon I have ever spent in Jerusalem and the best meal I have ever had there was after being invited home for lunch by George Akra, a young goldsmith whose work is the finest to be found in the city. He and his father had made the jewel-studded dress sword and scabbard given as a wedding present by King Hussein to his brother, Prince Mohammed, and had just finished weeks of intricate work on a new crown for a bishop who had lost his original one somewhere on the way to a conference in Athens.

The family's old home and workshop had been on the other side of the city and they had lost practically everything they had when they had to leave. But they had built up the business again to the point where they had recently been able to build a splendid villa on the outskirts of Jerusalem where hospitality knew no bounds. The mother of the family was a keen gardener and gave me some slips of a sweetly scented geranium that I had never seen before and which are now flourishing in my own garden.

Jerusalem's most famous street is the Via Dolorosa and every Friday afternoon the Franciscans lead a pilgrims' procession along it, starting at the Praetorium, Pilate's courtyard where Christ was condemned to death and the Roman washed his hands of the whole affair, and up past the first nine Stations of the Cross, to Calvary. The last five Stations are inside the Church of the Holy Sepulchre.

In this narrow, cobble-stoned Way of the Cross, Christian history rubs shoulders with the twentieth century for the street winds through some of the Old City's fascinating bazaars. You can shop for just about anything in the little booths that line it – fine golden rings and bracelets, brocades woven from gold and silver thread in Damascus, plastic shoes made in Italy, washing machines from Germany, Japanese transistor radios, Swiss cameras and watches, zinc buckets, carved olive-wood camels, hand-painted church candles, fish, cheese, olives, dried beans and chick-peas, fresh garlic and parsley and dozens of different kinds of breads and pastries. You have only to ask and whatever it is you are looking

Their first visit to England since their marriage—July 1962

King Hussein's sons: Prince
Abdullah (right), now aged four,
and Prince Feisal, three

A charming photograph of
Prince Abdullah

From the family album: (standing, from the left) Prince Mohammed, his
wife, Princess Ferial, Crown Prince Hassan, Princess Basma, Princess
Muna, King Hussein and Princess Alya. (seated) Queen Zein, the Queen
Mother, with Prince Feisal and Prince Abdullah

for will be found. And if you have asked at the wrong shop they will send a boy to show you the way to the right one.

In the spring there will be pedlars selling soft green almonds, a traditional Middle Eastern appetiser. Mounds of these delicately pale green nuts being sold from trays or barrows in the streets mean as much to the Arabs as the first primroses do to us; that spring is here at last.

In the autumn the booths will be garlanded with enormous bunches of fresh dates hanging on their slender stems like amber and cornelian beads. There are many kinds of dates and connoisseurs can tell them at a glance as we can a Cox's Orange Pippin apple from a Granny Smith or a Beauty of Bath, but I prefer the juicy, mahogany coloured ones although they are not as eye-catching as the golden.

At any time of the year you can taste a slice of *knaffe*, a honeyed cornmeal cake that is sold from great wooden trays, or a 'sandwich' made from spiced, ground meat, fried aubergines, or marrows, tomatoes and onions, all stuffed inside a warm round of freshly baked flat Arab bread.

In the heat of the summer the lemonade seller parades the street ringing a bell, stopping every time he finds a customer, to bend forward from the waist and deftly pour out a cupful from the brightly polished and elaborately decorated tank he carries strapped to his chest. Every few yards you can stop for a coffee or a glass of sweet tea and try one of the dozens of different kinds of pastries being made on the spot, some crisp and puffy like lightweight doughnuts, some like rounds of shortbread, but stuffed with nuts and spices and shaped in carved wooden moulds before being baked, and some made from paper-thin pastry layered with almonds and honey.

Every time the very active Municipality of Jerusalem starts on a plan of improving the facilities of the city, even if it is just to widen a street or lay a drain, the Department of Antiquities *must* be called in, because there is no knowing what the workmen's picks and spades are going to bring to light.

The most recent discoveries, two Crusader chapels, twelve feet below the threshold on the east and west sides of the Damascus Gate, were completely unexpected finds. The Municipality had decided to make the approach to the Gate, rebuilt in the sixteenth century by the Turkish Sultan Suleiman the Magnificent, even more impressive by building a piazza in front of the entrance and exposing the massive Roman defence walls beneath it.

During the digging on the western side of the Gate, the remains of stone walls, their plastered surface frescoed with haloed figures, and what is probably the site of an altar, were found. The faces of the figures had been deliberately chipped out, probably by the Tartars after they invaded Jerusalem in the thirteenth century, but there were enough details left, such as fragments of haloes, drapes and a banner, to show that they must have been paintings of saints.

The twelfth-century chapel had been built over a cistern which was used as a reserve water supply by the Crusaders, and had been completely buried up to the level of the present city wall of Jerusalem, also built by Suleiman. Archaeologists think that this chapel might be the Church of St Abraham which, according to Crusader chronicles, existed in this area, but has been lost for centuries.

A few months after this discovery another chapel was found on the eastern side, also well below the present level, and in it a great stone block carved with the Cross of Lorraine. The line of the Crusaders' city wall was found too, running parallel to the present sixteenth-century wall, but about thirty metres outside it and the present site of the Damascus Gate. Until this excavation it has always been assumed that Suleiman built his wall and gate on the same line as the wall built by the Crusaders five centuries before.

The foundations of the wall built by Hadrian in the second century when he refounded the city and called it Aelia Capitolania, have also been uncovered and from the time that this Roman wall was built to the time of the Crusaders, there is plenty of evidence of an uninterrupted succession of more than twenty road levels.

The wall around Jerusalem has fallen many times and to many

invaders, and the present one, Suleiman's, is pockmarked with the machine-gun fire of the last time the city was a battle-ground, during the Arab-Jewish war in 1948–9. Barbed wire runs along the top of the wall on the south and western sides which divide the Old City from modern Jerusalem and three gates in this stretch of the wall, New Gate, Jaffa Gate and Zion Gate, have been closed since 1948. Patrols of the Arab Army look out from their sand-bagged posts on the walls, across to no man's land and into 'the other side'. Four gates still leading through the wall into the Old City are Damascus Gate, Herod's Gate, St Stephen's Gate and the Dung Gate.

The first time I visited Jerusalem I was taken to a shell-blasted house on the edge of no man's land which was being used as a sorting centre for the bales of blankets and clothes that are sent from all over the world for the Palestine refugees. Teams of women and girls were busy unpacking, shaking out, grading and mending dresses, suits, coats, sweaters and underwear for men, women and children. I saw a beautifully handknitted baby's layette in one bundle and a collection of warm, long-sleeved nightgowns in another. The peasant women prize these night-gowns particularly. They wear them under their long dresses for extra warmth and can push their heavy dress sleeves up out of the way of their household chores without leaving their arms im-modestly bare.

'We can use unlimited numbers of sweaters and warm night-gowns,' I was told, 'and handknitted squares that we can put to-gether to make babies' blankets that are as warm as pie. Scotland is particularly good at sending these, and we are very grateful.'

One of the supervisors spotted an almost new, dark, pin-striped suit and instantly earmarked it for 'the general'. 'He was an important official at one time and still has tremendous pride in the way he dresses, even though all his clothes are now someone else's cast-offs,' she explained. 'He badly needs a warm suit for the winter. And that's something you might remind people about if you are going to write about us. A lot of people think of Jordan as a hot country, and forget that it can be bitterly cold in some

51

places, particularly in Jerusalem in the winter. They very kindly send us their unwanted summer clothes, but tend to think we don't need warm clothes too.'

She walked across to a window and looked out to a well-built stone house 'on the other side'. 'My grandfather built that house and I was born there. Now I believe there are three or four Jewish families living in it.' She spoke without bitterness, in a matter-of-fact kind of way. She, too, was a dispossessed refugee, but lucky in that she had found a job to keep her hands and her heart busy.

Bethlehem

THE OLD ROAD from Jerusalem to Bethlehem is now 'on the other side', so a new and longer road had to be built, winding eleven miles through the Judean hills instead of the former four.

Barbed wire divides the crest of the hill that is to the right of the road as you leave the city wall of Jerusalem and plunge down through the Kidron Valley, past the Pool of Siloam where Christ opened the eyes of the man who was born blind.

'See that hill?' says your taxi driver, pointing towards the barbed wire. 'That is on the other side. This hill is ours. Those two houses there are in no man's land and up there behind those trees are the headquarters of the United Nations.'

The road dips and twists through the hills like a fun-fair switchback and already motorists are demanding that a newer, straighter way to Bethlehem should be built. But on every crest you get a panoramic view of Judea and within minutes you are passing through the terraced olive groves of Sur Bahir from where you get your first glimpse of Bethlehem.

'Up there, almost on the border, is the Monastery of St Elias, belonging to the Greek Orthodox Church.' We had arrived at a road junction, the point where the new road to Bethlehem cuts across the old. The monastery stands a few yards up the disused road like a stranded whale on a deserted beach and is built on the site where legend says the Prophet Elias rested during his flight from the vengeful Queen Jezebel.

A little way further along the new road is the Tomb of Rachel who died giving birth to Benjamin while on her way to Bethlehem

53

(the Bible then called it Ephrata) with her husband Jacob. Here the road forks right to Hebron, the ancient city which was David's first capital and where six of his sons, including Absolom, were born.

For a while the Bethlehem road runs past fields that seem to grow nothing but stones and suddenly you realise the full significance of the Biblical seeds that fell on stony ground, for even twentieth-century farming methods have not been able to do much more with these fields than they could two thousand years ago. One of them is covered with strange little grey pebbles, so remarkable that a legend has grown around them. One day a man was sowing chick-peas in the field and Christ, who was passing by, asked him what he was doing. 'Sowing stones,' lied the man, and the answer was, 'Then you will reap stones.' And when the time came for the man to reap his harvest, he found nothing but petrified peas – his bitter reward for telling a lie. For generations this field has been called the Field of the Grey Peas because of this story.

Then you are back in hilly farmland where olives, almonds, peaches and vines grow in the ancient terraces and the low vines lie horizontally across the dark red earth, all pointing in the same direction as if bent that way by a constant wind.

A great, bent pine tree stands in the square outside Bethlehem's Church of the Nativity and was probably the first Christmas tree, for during Christmas week it is hung with coloured lights and competes with the much newer neon-lit star that has been wired to the top of the church. The stone walls of the church are as thick as those of a fortress and everyone must bend down to enter through the low door – the Door of Humility. Unlike the great church in Jerusalem, it was not sacked by the Persians when they overran Palestine in the seventh century AD. Your guide will tell you that they spared the church because they saw one of the walls was decorated with a mosaic of the Three Kings, dressed as Persians.

Coloured glass balls, the originals of the glittering baubles that we hang on our Christmas trees, are suspended from the ceiling

of the Basilica among the beautiful silver filigree lamps. Beneath
a wooden trapdoor set into the stone flags of the floor you can look
at the fourth-century Byzantine mosaics that covered the floor of
the first church, built by St Helena, which was pulled down and
re-built in the sixth century by Emperor Justinian. Although the
Crusaders altered it a little, it is Justinian's church which still
stands over the cave where Christ was born and the manger in
which Mary laid Him.

Not far from the Church of the Nativity, women come down to
the Well of Mary to fill their water jars, just as they have done
since Biblical times, except nowadays the jar is more likely to be a
large petrol jerrican than a hand-thrown pot or a goatskin.

The housewives of Bethlehem are dressed much the same as
Mary might have been too, in long black or dark blue robes embroidered across the bodice and in panels down the skirt, with
patterns of brightly coloured flowers : the scarlet anemone, white
and pink cyclamen, hollyhock, buttercup and the silvery Star of
Bethlehem, that turn the brown fields and valleys around the
town into a rainbowed carpet in the spring. Since Crusader times,
the wives of Bethlehem have added a black velvet jacket encrusted,
if they can afford it, with gold embroidery, and a tall, conical hat,
the *shatwah,* which is draped with a white gauze veil and tied on
under the chin with a necklace of gold dowry coins. Apart from
the dowry necklace, which is purely Middle Eastern, and their
own addition, the headdress has not changed since it was the
height of medieval fashion among the wives of the Crusader
Knights.

At Christmas Bethlehem becomes a vast dormitory, just as it
was that first Christmas, and anyone who has not booked a bed at
an hotel or in one of the convents, church hostels or private homes,
will find there is 'no room at the inn.' Thousands attend the
simple Protestant Christmas Eve service which is held in the
YMCA's plantation of pine trees around a large cave. After the
service everyone joins in a traditional supper of 'shepherd's meat',
flat Arab bread and roast lamb.

This could have been the field in which the shepherds were

55

watching their flock on the night they were visited by the angels while sheltering, perhaps, in the cave from the cold winds that sweep the Judean hills in the winter. But there are two other traditional shepherds' fields on the outskirts of Bethlehem. The one that belongs to the Greek Orthodox Church is planted with olive trees, has a little chapel built over another cave and the remains of a much earlier monastery and church. The other belongs to the Roman Catholics and was once the site of a thriving monastery farm. Olive presses, cisterns, silos and grottoes that might have been used for storing crops have been found and the remains of a fourth-century church with two altars and mosaic inscriptions.

A modern, imaginative chapel has been built in the shape of a tent on this site. Inside its alcoves are painted with lovely frescoes by Noni, showing the story of the shepherds. The Star of Bethlehem glitters in a dark blue sky and pairs of fat-cheeked cherubs hover above the bewildered shepherds and their sheep as they follow the Star to the Manger.

In Bethlehem, while shopping for a carved olive-wood set of Nativity figures, I met Mr Elias Freij, a local craftsman who makes and sells them and who also has a mother-of-pearl factory that has belonged to his family for three hundred years.

After a cup of coffee and a long deliberation in his shop over the most appealing set of figures, for they all differ slightly in the rich grain of the wood and the expressions on their faces, Mr Freij took me to see his workshops where one hundred thousand mother-of-pearl beads in thirty-six different sizes and shapes are made every week then strung into rosaries that go all over the world, 'but particularly to Ireland, Italy and America'. Intricate mosaic covers for Bibles and missals and for olive-wood boxes are made of slivers of mother-of-pearl fitted together in delicate patterns. Beautiful crosses, brooches, earrings and necklaces are painstakingly hand-carved with tiny saws and chisels, sometimes as many as a thousand careful strokes going to make one small piece.

There are other workshops like Mr Freij's for the mother-of-pearl craft, which was introduced to Bethlehem in the sixteenth century by the Franciscans, is the town's most important industry and earns a substantial amount for Jordan's economy. It was in Bethlehem that the panorama of Jerusalem, carved out of olive wood and mother-of-pearl and presented to Pope Paul as a souvenir of his pilgrimage to the Holy Land, was made.

But the most remarkable thing about this thriving industry is that all these mother-of-pearl masterpieces are made from off-cuts bought from button factories and a Sheffield firm that still makes pearl-handled knives. What will happen to Bethlehem's unique workshops when plastic buttons and stainless steel really take over I do not know.

Martha and Mary's Village

BARBED WIRE AND no man's land do not scar the road to Bethany, Jericho and Amman, which leaves Jerusalem by St Stephen's Gate on the east side of the city. A large rock outside the Gate is the legendary site of the stoning of St Stephen, the first Christian martyr. But the Arabs call the Gate *Bab Sitti Maryam,* the Gate of the Lady Mary, for just inside it is the Church of St Anne, built over the site of the birthplace of the Virgin Mary in the house of her parents, Anne and Joachim. Outside, the Gate looks across to Gethsemane and the Mount of Olives and the road dips down into the Kidron Valley (its Arab name, *Wadi Sitti Maryam*), past the Virgin's Tomb, over which the Crusaders built a church to replace a much older one which was in ruins.

Bethany is still a pretty little village, just over a mile away from Jerusalem, and there the Franciscans have built a new church on the site of the house of Martha and Mary.

A tiny, bearded monk met me at the door and in a mixture of German, French, English and Latin, explained that the new church had been built on the foundations of two older ones, the first Byzantine, the second Crusader. He showed me an ancient olive press like a giant wooden screw, which is carefully propped up in a cave in the rocky hill beside the church. It looked old enough to have been used by the Crusaders, but I could not discover whether or not they had pressed their oil with it for, by then, the little monk's home-made esperanto had petered out and we could find no more words in common.

The Tomb of Lazarus is another, deeper cave, further up the

same hillside. Outside an old man was playing on a reed pipe, a pile of them for sale on the ground at his feet. He was also selling candles to anyone who wanted to go inside, for the Jordanians, while caring scrupulously well for all the holy places, have resisted any impulse to 'improve' them. Had this been any other country, an electric light would have been switched on at once to illuminate the slab on which Lazarus was lying when he was raised from the dead.

My candle flickered madly in the cold air of the cave and I had to feel carefully along the worn surfaces of the steps carved out of the rock as I went deeper and deeper.

I did not stay long. I was glad to get back to the bright sunshine after a few minutes and to hurry down the rocky path, past goats and children, to the little garden full of lilies and sweet scented stocks that the Franciscans have planted outside their church.

Perhaps there was something to be said for electric light after all. But the heretic thought had gone by the time I was back in the car. A pair of sensible flat-heeled shoes was all I had really needed. . . .

The Oldest Town in the World

MORE THAN ANYWHERE else in Jordan I had wanted to see
Jericho, the world's oldest town and the lowest, since it is eight
hundred and twenty-five feet below sea level. Jericho, whose great
stone watch tower is four thousand years older than the oldest
pyramid, whose walls fell to the blast of Joshua's trumpets and
whose green oasis of date palms and cool groves of lemons, oranges
and bananas were a love gift to the fascinating Cleopatra from
both Julius Caesar and Mark Antony – Herod the Great had
leased it between lovers.

More than once I had seen its emerald sheen in the distance
across the moon landscape of the arid white salt hummocks that
surround the Dead Sea, as I branched off to Amman on the
road out of Jerusalem. I had eaten the small, deliciously sweet
bananas that grow in Jericho all the year round and juicy tomatoes, lettuces and cucumbers that come from the town's lush
market gardens watered by the spring that Elisha sweetened two
thousand eight hundred years ago by casting in a handful of salt.
But I always had to hurry past on my way to keep some appoint-
ment or other in Amman until one Friday, the Moslem holiday
and Jordan's weekly day of rest.

The day before, I had visited the Palace in Amman with one
of my newspaper's photographers to make arrangements for
photographing Prince Abdullah, the newly born son of King
Hussein and Princess Muna, and Saturday was fixed as the day.
The King, who had been out riding, came into the room as we
were leaving the Princess and asked us what our plans were for

60

Friday. We had none, so he invited us up to Amman airfield in the afternoon to watch the kart races.

'What about the morning though, is there anywhere you would like to visit that you haven't already seen? Have you been to Jericho for instance?' the King then asked. It was a heaven-sent opportunity and I took it, before Bill, the photographer, had time to think.

Promptly at nine the next morning, a large and impressive sergeant of the Jordanian Army arrived at the hotel in one of the royal cars and drove us off to Jericho at such a speed we might have been chasing a passing show due to fade away in minutes, instead of going to look at a town that had been there for the last ten thousand years. We left the hills of Amman and plunged down into the Jordan Valley, crossing the river at King Abdullah Bridge, and the distant, bright blue shimmer of the Dead Sea rushed towards us. Bill spotted a cluster of Bedouin tents on the shore and a boy with a flock of sheep. 'Marvellous picture,' he yelled, reaching for his camera, 'get him to stop.' But we were going so fast the black tents were half a mile behind us before the sergeant pulled up. 'Never mind, I'll get it on the way back,' said Bill, already growing as philosophical as any Arab, after only two days away from Fleet Street.

Behind us we could see the towers of Jerusalem outlined against the sky on the crest of the Judean hills, over two thousand five hundred feet above us but only twenty-two miles away. Up there, I knew, there would be a cool mountain breeze but in the valley it was getting hotter and hotter as we dropped down, almost, it seemed, to the centre of the earth. Ahead we could see the palm groves, farmlands, lovely stone-built villas and rose gardens of modern Jericho, and covering the sides of the hills outside the town, almost to the foot of the towering Mount of Temptation, were two of the biggest refugee camps in the whole of Jordan.

We asked the sergeant to let us see something of them and he stopped outside the office of the Camp Director, himself a refugee, who told us there were sixty thousand Palestinian refugees living in the area, most of them jobless and relying for their ex-

61

istence on UNWRA and various Church charities' rations, and a 'dole' of two shillings a day. 'But,' he added almost defiantly, 'our camps are cleaner than the West Side of New York and perhaps even the East Side.' From what we could see we could believe him, but we had no time that morning to go on a tour of inspection. We had set out to see old and new Jericho and we had to be back in Amman by 1.30 pm for the start of the kart races.

Donkeys jostled for road space with cars and jeeps in the main streets of modern Jericho. A small boy sauntered past with a stem of ripe bananas draped over his head like an outlandish bonnet. Black-robed and black-skinned women with wristfuls of gold and silver bangles and sometimes gold nose-rings, descendants of the Negro soldiers left one hundred and twenty-five years ago by the army of Ibrahim Pasha, shopped for fresh fruit and vegetables, joints of goat and camel meat and pots of thick, creamy *laban*, the delicious local yoghourt which is made from goat's milk. It was strange to see the *laban* being taken out of a modern refrigerator while, right alongside, oranges, beans, lettuces and dark green water melons sliced to show their juicy coral flesh were piled high on rush mats on the ground in a colourful, primitive sales display that was old in Bible days.

The Jericho of the Canaanites lies under a high mound, the Tell al Sultan, just outside the new town. The Arab word *tell* is used to describe an artificial hill as opposed to *jebel*, a mountain, and often indicates the site of an ancient settlement. We scrambled up the rocky, dusty slope and from the top could see modern Jericho lying in the plain below us, the sparkling waters of the Dead Sea three miles away and the Mount of Temptation with a monastery clinging to its dark brown side like a lizard on a wall.

Looking down into the excavations the guide pointed out the distinct lines of three town foundations, embedded in the sliced side of the *tell* one above the other like layers in a rich gateau. The oldest, he said, was built nearly ten thousand years ago. The time when the walls came tumbling down before Joshua – although the archaeologists think it was more likely to have been a well-timed earthquake than a trumpet blast that did the trick – was comparatively not so long ago, less than four thousand years away.

A massive stone watch tower, hollowed out inside to hold a staircase of wide stone steps, lies against the wall and now that it has been dug out of the rubble of centuries looms over the excavations like an ancient threat. It was spell-binding to realise that this tower was as old to the Egyptians when they started to build their first pyramid as Stonehenge now is to us.

It must have struck a chill fear in the hearts of even the aggressive and confident Israelites when their captain, Joshua, pointed it out and told them they were going to take it by storm. And what a disastrously false sense of security it must have given the citizens of Jericho as they climbed up inside to view from the pinnacle the black tents of the Hebrew tribes massing over the slopes on which the refugee camps now stand.

When the tower was excavated a few years ago twelve skeletons were found in the passage at its foot, but Kathleen Kenyon, in her fascinating book, *Digging up Jericho,* has decided that these could not have been the tower's last heroic defenders since the floor level of the passage had risen to within two feet of the roof by the time the bodies were put in. By then it must have been nothing more than a convenient hole for disposing of twelve dead men.

Long before the tented Israelites attacked Jericho the townspeople were living a comparatively elegant life. The floors and walls of their houses were smoothly plastered, their stools, tables and beds were carved from cedar, willow and tamarisk woods, they had alabaster bowls, decorated pottery jars, jugs and pedestal-based goblets, woven rush mats for their floors and wooden platters for their food. They combed their hair with wooden combs that were meticulously cut with bronze saws, kept their toilet things in pretty little boxes inlaid with delicate patterns of carved bone and wore bronze rings set with scarabs on their fingers, coloured bead necklaces and gold bracelets. The housewives baked their bread in mud ovens shaped like molehills – the kind you can still see Arab housewives using in Jordan.

In the mornings and evenings they went down with their water jars to the fresh water spring, later to be associated with the prophet Elisha, just as the women from the refugee camps do to-day. What the Canaanite housewives called their spring we do not know, but since Old Testament times it has been known as Elisha's Fountain. The water is still as cool and good to drink as it must have been after the prophet flung in a handful of salt to sweeten it when the men of Jericho said to him, 'Behold, I pray thee, the situation of this city is pleasant, as my lord seeth : but the water is naught and the ground barren.'

I have been back to Jericho many times since that day and one late afternoon, after almost being blown down from the top of the Tell al Sultan by a sudden *khamsin,* the hot, blinding sandstorm that whips across from the Arabian desert in the spring, I walked down to Elisha's Fountain as the women were filling their water carriers. One of them scooped up a cool draught of water in a plastic mug and handed it to me, and nothing had ever tasted so good. But for that twentieth-century mug and the petrol jerri-cans that were being filled from the spring, I could have been back in Old Testament days for the women were all dressed in the flowing, embroidered robes that must have been familiar to Elisha.

Archaeologists are beginning to think it could have been this spring and the nearby River Jordan which inspired Man to make the revolutionary discovery that he could live a settled life instead of wandering in search of food; that he could sow and harvest the wild grains he had always had to search for and could herd the wild animals he had always had to hunt.

It is possible that further excavations might one day prove that Jericho was the world's first settled community, the place where civilisation began, as they have already proved that it is the oldest town in the world yet to have been found.

The Lowest Spot on Earth

THE ROAD THAT passes Elisha's Fountain leads to the foot of the Mount of Temptation and skirts the ancient Canaanite town and the greater part of the modern refugee camp. The mountain's Latin name, Quarantana, recalls the climax of Christ's forty days of solitude in the Judean wilderness when Satan took Him to the mountain top to tempt Him with 'all the kingdoms of the world and the glory of them'. The mountainside is honey-combed with caves where hermits lived in the early days of Christianity, and half-way up is a Greek Orthodox monastery, built nearly a hundred years ago, where you can rest for a while before going further.

It is a hard climb to the summit, on which stands another, smaller monastery and the ruins of a Byzantine church. From the top there is a fabulous view of the Jordan Valley as far as snow-capped Mount Hermon in Syria in one direction, and in the other, the deceptively fresh looking waters of the Dead Sea with a pink and mauve backcloth of the Mountains Moab and Gilead.

Almost at your feet are the ancient and modern towns of Jericho and a little beyond them, the green-fringed curve of the Jordan River at Makhadet al Hijla – the Ford of the Partridge – one of the sites claimed as the place where St John baptised Christ and where you can now buy a bottle of Jordan water that has been specially treated by the monks of a nearby monastery to stay sweet so that it can be taken all over the world for family baptisms. If you fill your own bottle, as many people do, the water will have to be used within weeks for the organic matter in it soon turns it cloudy.

One thousand two hundred and fifty million tons of sweet

E

Jordan water pour into the Dead Sea each year, carrying with
them the mineral salts that have made this strange sea six times
saltier than the ocean. Sometimes fish and other living things get
swept into the Sea too, and are quickly stifled by the dense and
salty water. Unlike the fish on the famous sixth century AD mosaic
map of Palestine at Madaba, which are shown swimming back
up stream at the point where the Jordan flows into the Dead Sea,
the real fish cannot escape their fate.

So sinister is this Sea's reputation there is a superstition that a
bird cannot fly over it and live, and there is reason in this when
you think of the dense evaporation above it every day, caused by
the blazing sun. But I have seen birds dare it, many times, and
always get away with it.

Bathing in the Dead Sea is like making your way through a
great bowl of warm beef soup, for although it looks invitingly
blue, clear and sparkling from a distance, once in, it is pale brown
and sticky. By the time you have waded in up to the waist it has
floated you off your feet and you are bobbing around like a cork.
Try to swim and your behind and legs will float up out of the water
in a most undignified way. It is the only sea in the world you can
swim on, not in, but even this is hard work. The only thing to do
is to give up any idea of exercise and just float nonchalantly
around on your back, like everyone else is doing, and have fun
watching other first-timers come in and try to swim in the usual
fashion; for no one seems to believe what they have heard about
the Dead Sea until they have tried it for themselves.

Herod the Great, who had a winter palace built at Jericho,
used to float in these waters every day in the hope that the mineral
salts would cure his various diseases, and he seemed to have more
than most men. Even today the Dead Sea is still recommended as
a cure-all and there is no doubt that it can be beneficial. My
husband, who has a stiff knee – a war relic – said it had never
felt better after he had floated around in the water for half an
hour. I have been told that the water cleanses and strengthens
the eyes, but this I would not recommend, for even a drop stings
sharply and can 'blind' for a short while.

Linger on the beach to sunbathe when you come out and within five minutes you will turn into a pillar of salt as Lot's wife did at a spot not very far from where you are enjoying yourself. You must take a fresh water shower quickly, for even before you have crossed the beach to the shower rooms, the desert sun will have turned the salt on your skin to a glistening white frost.

A modern winter resort hotel has been built on the beach just off the road to Jericho. The sign outside welcomes you to 'the lowest spot on earth'. It is a favourite weekend retreat for people living in Amman and Jerusalem and in the winter there is the added fun of camel and horse racing in the sports stadium nearby.

If you are there for the day you can hire a towel, leave your clothes in a locker and have a 'swim' in the Sea, a fresh shower, then lunch on the beach under a striped umbrella and reflect that somewhere under the placid, buoyant waters might lie the wicked cities of Sodom and Gomorrah that disappeared in a rain of brimstone and fire. Archaeologists have searched the Dead Sea for them, sending divers down into the murky waters in specially weighted diving suits to prevent them from bobbing back to the surface, but have found nothing.

Other scholars believe that the cities might have been on the Lisam peninsula, a tongue of land that juts out into the Dead Sea below the Mountains of Moab on the eastern shore. A recent excavation has uncovered a huge necropolis there containing at least twenty thousand tombs and dating from about 2500 BC. Some of the underground burial chambers had been disturbed, but others were completely untouched, and the excavators were the first to look inside them since the day they were sealed four and a half thousand years ago.

Among the piles of bones they found figurines representing fertility gods and goddesses, a crescent-shaped battle axe, copper daggers, beads, plaques, jugs, lamps and plates. The marks of the tools the masons used to cut the tombs out of the limestone were still quite clear.

But so far, the two cities that were last seen in Abraham's day are still missing without real trace. If you go out from the hotel

67

in one of the glass-bottomed boats, you might fancy you can see something way down below.

But mostly once offshore, eyes are kept scanning the waters for Jewish patrol boats, because the armistice line runs across the Dead Sea as well as the land. There is an Arab patrol station near the Dead Sea Hotel and one morning we were invited to join a small party on one of the patrol boats for a sail across to Zarka Ma'in at the foot of the Mountains of Moab, where we were planning to swim, picnic and soak ourselves in the pools that are filled by hot natural springs.

Ten of these hot mineral springs gush out of the steep cleft of the Wadi Zarka Ma'in. Some are pleasantly warm and relaxing, others too hot for comfort, and all have a therapeutic value famous since Roman times. Naturally, Herod was a regular visitor to these springs, and used to be carried from another of his palaces at Machareus (now Makhaiyat) down the mountain side in a litter to bathe in the pools. It was at Machareus, southwest of Madaba, that Salome danced and was rewarded with the head of John the Baptist. The Romans built a landing stage on the beach which they called Callirhoe, so that they could sail across from the Jericho side. As the level of the Dead Sea rose over the centuries the wooden quay was submerged, but recently, because of the diversion of the Jordan waters for irrigation and the commercial extraction of salts from the sea, the level has dropped enough to uncover it again.

The contrast between this side of the Sea, its pebbly beach backed by sandstone mountains so vividly coloured they might have been painted, and the sterile, salt-white shore from which we had sailed, was dramatic. Little but camel thorn and creeping succulents powdered with grey dust grow on the side we had left, but we stepped ashore at Zarka Ma'in in front of a green, well-watered valley and scrambled through a jungle of thick scrub – tamarisks, thorns and tall, silver feathered grass – to look for the wadi's springs.

The boys of a Bedouin family whose tents were pitched in the wadi ran ahead of us and shinned to the top of a rocky spur where they stayed all morning enjoying their balcony view of our beach party. By ten o'clock, it was already too hot to climb, so we gave up the idea of going up the mountainside to see if we could pick out Mount Nebo, from whose summit Moses looked over the Promised Land. We found a cave on the beach which made a perfect changing room and foiled the inquisitive small boys perched over our heads. After floating around in the Sea for a bit, we soaked blissfully in the warm mineral pools and washed the salt off our skins.

We ate our picnic of flat Arab bread stuffed with spiced meat, tomatoes and onions, and debated whether or not the plan for developing this lovely, lonely place as a modern spa was a good idea. For centuries the Arabs have used the wadi as a natural spa and hunting ground. It is still full of wild partridge and has a reputation for curing, among other things, barrenness. One Jordanian I know in London told me he could remember being taken as a small boy, by his parents and childless aunt and uncle, on a camping weekend to the springs where his aunt soaked for hours in the waters while his father and uncle shot partridge. 'She had a baby not long afterwards, but whether the springs had much more to do with it than help her relax and feel well, I do not know,' he said.

The plans for developing the wadi include a new road from Madaba, the nearest town, which is in the centre of the fertile plain of Moab. The existing road from Madaba to Zarka Ma'in is narrow, rocky and hard going, especially when it reaches the edge of the mountain range and plunges down to the wadi and the beach. The thick bush around the heads of the mountainside springs and their pools will be cleared and a small, modern hotel will be put up on the wild and beautiful little beach, which even in the winter when there is snow on the Judean hills, a few miles away, is always warm and sunny. There will also be a regular boat service across the Dead Sea from the Jericho side.

The partridges and the Bedouin boys will migrate to another part of the land, and the absolute peace of this secret place will disappear too. But with tasteful development of the kind that is going on in other parts of Jordan, I cannot think of a more naturally perfect spot than Zarka Ma'in for relaxing and recovering from our Western rat-race. The Romans, who were connoisseurs of spas and made the most of their recuperative powers, used to think the same about this lovely valley at the edge of the Dead Sea.

From the Dead Sea Hotel it is only a half-hour drive away to the Qumran caves where the Dead Sea scrolls were found in 1947 by a Bedouin shepherd who was looking for a lost sheep.

Your car will bump along a wild and dusty track by the shores of the Dead Sea, startling flocks of swallow-like birds that swoop up and away into the sun. It will stop beside a little wooden booth selling fizzy drinks and from here you must walk up a rocky slope to the top of a plateau where the low ruins of two thousand years old Kirbet Qumran stand on the site of an even older Iron Age fortress. At first, the ruins are difficult to spot. They almost merge into the desolate pale brown landscape and until you actually reach them seem to be yet another cluster of desert rocks that have been whittled into fanciful shapes by sun, salt and wind-driven sand.

But you can walk into kitchens, an assembly hall, refectory and scriptorium, see the huge reservoirs carved out of the solid rock in which rainwater from the steep cliffs adjoining the Wadi Qumran was stored. You can trace the stone aqueducts by which the water was conducted from the base of the cliffs to the reservoirs within the settlement and walk cobbled streets that were laid by men forty generations ago.

If you are there in Jordan's brief spring the rocky ground will be carpeted with low patches of wild flowers, some of them so tiny that they need to be lifted close to appreciate their intricate beauty and delicate colour. But be careful where you pick, for there are scorpions and snakes about, although it is most unlikely that you will see them. What you will see are scores of large grasshoppers that open their wings to display a flash of brilliant vermilion as they hop out of reach. There will be hawks circling around the cliffs and over the deep wadi and if you are lucky you might catch a glimpse of a wild mountain cat, for even this most arid of deserts is not empty of wild life.

70

Kirbet Qumran was the lonely desert retreat of an intensely religious community which has been identified through the scrolls as the Essenes. They were an austere Jewish sect who devoted their lives to studying the writings of the Old Testament and praying for the coming of the Messiah.

In their scriptorium the scribes sat at white-plastered, mud-brick benches to copy onto leather and papyrus and plaques of thin copper their books of the Old Testament, their own commentaries on them, their hymns, liturgies and accounts of the daily life of their community. From their plateau they were able to gaze across the Dead Sea and the wilderness around it to the Mountains of Moab and the fleshpots of nearby Jericho. But they lived in frugal poverty, in idealistic equality with the same shares of what little they had for all.

Did Christ go to Qumran? He was not far away when He climbed the Mount of Temptation and He visited Jericho many times. The more that is being discovered from piecing together and deciphering the scrolls of the Essenes the more their philosophy and background corresponds with those of the early Christians.

In the spring of 68 AD the Essenes hurriedly cleared their scriptorium council chamber of their precious scrolls and hid them in the deep caves that riddle the sides of the surrounding rocky cliffs like holes in a pigeon loft, for the Roman Tenth Legion, on a punitive expedition to Jerusalem to quell the First Jewish Revolt, was on its way to Qumran.

It seems the devout and gentle Essenes never returned to Qumran after the Roman raiding party left, for the place was deserted for over fifty years until its ruins were temporarily used as a hiding place by the rebels during the Second Jewish Revolt. When this was crushed by Titus, the desert took over Qumran for nearly two thousand years and only the wandering Bedouins knew it, as a shelter for their flocks.

So far more than six hundred different manuscripts have been found in the Qumran caves and more might still be there, waiting to be brought up into the sun. It is going to take years for the team of scholars and scientists to repair, clean, and translate the thousands of scroll fragments now housed in the Scrollery in the Palestine Archaeological Museum in Jerusalem. Many of the leather and papyrus scrolls were in fragile pieces after centuries of dirt, damp and the nibblings of rats and insects, and the writing was darkened to the point where it could be read only by the help of infra-red light. The copper scrolls, which were made of riveted sheets of thin copper that had been rolled for storing, had oxidised and broken. Eventually they had to be cut into strips and pieced together again before the text could be read. They were found to contain lists of hiding places for hoards of treasure and ever since hopeful parties have been going off on treasure hunting expeditions, but so far without any luck.

But the scrolls themselves are a treasure beyond price, and you can see some of them, and the pottery, seats and benches, with inkpots still containing traces of the carbon ink used by the Essene scribes, in a special exhibition room in the Palestine Museum in Jerusalem.

Modern Miracle in the Desert

IT IS MORE in Jericho than anywhere else in Jordan that the air is charged with the possibility of miracles. The laws of nature have been flouted here so often, from the time Man turned from a hunter into a farmer, to the day when Christ gave back sight to Bartimaeus, the blind beggar, that the newest miracle, now blossoming in the salt-soaked desert for everyone to see, almost seems a logical step in the history of this place. Two thousand acres of sun-baked, salt-encrusted land that has never grown anything but tufts of camel scrub because it is outside the fertile reach of Elisha's spring, has been turned into a model farm supporting nearly two hundred orphaned refugees and producing enough surplus milk, eggs, fruit and vegetables to sell in local markets and even export to the Persian Gulf.

Bartimaeus's faith produced one miracle, and the faith of Musa Bey Alami has produced another. In 1948, during the Arab-Jewish war, Musa Bey, Cambridge graduate, lawyer and former Palestine Government official, decided on a plan to give hope to at least some of the thousands of refugee children who had been orphaned in the fighting. He too was a refugee and had lost most of his property, but he still had some money of his own left and was holding funds belonging to the Arab Development Society which had been started some years before to help improve the living conditions of the peasant farmers in Palestine. The land the Society had acquired for setting up model villages was now on the other side of the armistice line.

Musa Bey's idea was to use this money he had to reclaim land that could be worked by refugee farmers who had lost their own, and to build a home on the farm for orphaned boys and a vocational school where those not inclined towards farming could be taught a trade. The Jordan Government gave him a concession of two thousand acres of desert between Jericho and the Dead Sea, that only he was convinced could be cultivated. He believed that water was to be found in this seemingly dead stretch of the Jordan Valley, even though every irrigation expert in the country thought he was wasting his time looking for it.

For six months, Musa Bey and a small group of associates and refugees who shared his faith, dug for water in the parched and salty ground. Their trial wells had to be drilled by hand because they could not afford machinery, and one day, after excavating to a depth of seventy five feet, they rested on their spades and wept. They had struck sweet water.

The next two years were spent washing the soil free of the sterilising salt with water brought up from the depths of the land, and planting rows of quick growing eucalyptus trees to shade the newly sown crops from the fierce desert sun. Modern machinery was acquired and more water found at varying levels and soon the farm was thriving. Then a start was made on the second of Musa Bey's plans, the vocational school and home for boys. Simple huts were built, eventually to be replaced by permanent living quarters, schoolrooms and workshops, and Musa Bey announced that the Jericho Arab Development Society was ready to take in the first batch of orphaned refugee boys.

This was the start of Jordan's 'Boys' Town', a place where boys with no home of their own can live for eight years, be given elementary education and then vocational training in farming, carpentry, shoe-making, weaving, motor mechanics and metal-work, so that they can eventually make their own way in the world. Many have done so since those early days. Boys from this school can now earn as much in Jordan as any high school graduate, and because they are trained to fill the gap between the administrator and the worker and do both jobs when necessary, they are in great demand. The school has a long waiting list, too, of jobs to be filled by the workshop trained boys not only in Jordan but also in the Persian Gulf and Beirut.

The third part of Musa Bey's plans was to help provide a livelihood for the people living in the frontier villages along the armistice line. Most of these villages have lost their farming lands and therefore their sustenance, and in some cases have also been deprived of their sources of water. All they have left on their side of no man's land are their houses. But as long as a man is clinging to his own home, he cannot be classed as a refugee and so cannot claim help from UNRWA. Many of these villagers were nearer to starvation and utter despair than the refugees who had moved into the camps until people like Musa Bey stretched out a hand.

Musa Bey's school at Jericho takes boys from these villages and gives them workshop training so that they can go home and teach others. The Society has also taught one thousand five hundred frontier village girls to develop their traditional skill of embroidering so that their work has a modern commercial value, and has opened a shop in Jerusalem, opposite the Ambassador Hotel, where the lovely things they make can be sold. Young women instructors go out from this Jerusalem headquarters to start craft centres in the villages and organise a supply of finished goods. Tablecloth and napkin sets made from hand-woven and hand-dyed fabrics and exquisitely worked in traditional cross-stitch patterns are perhaps the best sellers, and can be bought for a few pounds. Almost anywhere else in the world they would fetch six or seven times the amount, and I am surprised that some enterprising British shop has not yet discovered that here is a new source of supply for wedding gifts that will become family heirlooms.

Ever since Musa Bey's dream started to come true, he has wanted to build a permanent vocational training school for girls on the same lines as the boys' school. 'Of the school-age girls among the six hundred and fifty thousand refugees in Jordan, less than thirty per cent can get a place in school,' he told me the day I visited him at his home on the farm. 'But I cannot start a school for girls until I have a regular source of maintenance for the boys' school.

'We have been living from hand to mouth ever since we started this project in the Jordan Valley, and it has been a constant uphill fight. Profits from the sale of farm produce are put back into the Society, and we also have a Trust Fund, but not enough subscribers, for not enough people seem to know about us. We get support from various sources such as Interchurch Aid, Oxfam, the World Refugee Year Fund and the Friends of the Arab Development Society which is registered as a charity in England, but we have no regular, permanent income. It is never possible to budget ahead because we do not know how much to expect. It's much easier to find capital than to find maintenance to keep things going.'

Already the boys' school has been in danger of having to close through lack of funds, but Musa Bey and his colleagues have struggled on. He realises that what they are doing is only helping to plug a small hole in the flood of the refugees' despair.

'We are not here to solve any problem. We are here only to point the way as to how we think some of these great difficulties can be met,' he said. 'Many were against us when we first preached vocational training instead of academic; they were even against agricultural training, although we are mainly an agricultural country. Many believed that nothing could be done with this part of the Jordan Valley, but since we showed that it could be turned into fertile land, forty-five thousand acres around us have now been reclaimed by private enterprise.

'I believe that the Jordan Valley can easily support a new population of half-a-million people and supply food for many more, but it can only be done by extensively controlled farming. The trouble with we Arabs is that we are individualists. Arab farmers will not pull together, and in a scheme like this, group planning is most essential.'

I suspected there are other stumbling blocks too that might be preventing the arid land from being turned into a cornucopia— emotional and political ones that Musa Bey did not want to discuss. He sounded weary and disillusioned, this man who had found sweet water in the salty desert and seen a miracle blossom. It was obvious that many years of uphill battling had sapped his strength. But he has built up around him a strong team of young men who share his vision and have all of his own determination to keep it alive.

One of them showed me round the farm after I had said good-bye to Musa Bey Alami. 'Come and see our dairy,' he said. 'It's the most modern in the country. We milk on the herring-bone system and now, for the first time ever in Jordan, milk goes straight from the cow into the bottle without being touched by hand. Look at all this marvellous equipment; it was sent to us by the Ford Foundation and we are very proud of it. Already we have a big demand for milk supplies and can even produce homogenised milk, the first in the country. We have a shop in Amman to sell it and eventually we may find there is a call for us to start home-to-home milk deliveries.

'But look over here, this is our greatest treasure.'

It was a tiny black and white calf, born that morning, the first of the second generation of milch cows to be born on the farm, and surely a sign that Musa Bey Alami's modern miracle had taken firm root.

Moabites and Mosaics

THE GREEN PALM trees of Jericho's oasis are clearly marked on one of the most fascinating maps in the world, a mosaic picture map of Palestine, probably dating from the sixth century AD, that is in Madaba, a town on the ancient Moabite plain about twenty miles south of Amman.

The map was once part of the floor of an early Byzantine basilica over which the town's modern Greek Orthodox Church of St George has been built. It shows all the natural features of the land, the mountains, the rivers, the inland seas and the Mediterranean coast as well as the cities and villages built by man and quaint little pictures of contemporary life. There is a boat being rowed by sailors across the Dead Sea, fat fish swimming in the River Jordan, over which is a bridge. A gazelle is being stalked by a lion on the slopes of Mount Nebo and there is a wonderful, panoramic view of Jerusalem as it was in the days of Justinian. The walls and great gates of the city are clearly marked and so is a magnificent street of columns cutting through its centre from west to east. The remains of the column I had seen in the baker's shop outside the Church of the Holy Sepulchre had once been part of this splendid way.

To look at the map correctly, so that the sites marked on it fall in their proper place, you have to face towards the east. If the light in the church is bright enough, you can still trace the lovely colours the craftsmen used when they were constructing it — four subtle shades of red, at least five of green, and violet, blue, brown, white, cream, yellow, grey and black, all set in a background of white limestone.

78

It is possible that this unique mosaic map was the forerunner of the early medieval pictorial maps. Since it is one of the earliest known contemporary maps of Palestine, it has been of importance in helping to identify the sites of ancient towns.

If the church is not open, you have only to ring the bell above the main entrance to call the warden, although I hope by now someone has put a longer piece of rope on it. The last time I wanted to ring I had to get help in the shape of a small boy and quite a large policeman. Even the policeman was not tall enough to reach the frayed end, so the boy had to climb on his shoulders to do it, by which time we had gathered such a crowd of delighted onlookers that the warden was already on his way to see what all the fuss was about.

Modern Madaba is built on a layered hill which is all that is left of its ancient forerunners. The first mention of it is in the Bible's story of the Exodus at the point where the tribes of Israel, under Moses, had overrun the land of Moab and had 'laid them waste even unto Nophah, which reacheth unto Medeba'.

Not far from Madaba, to the north-west, is Mount Nebo, high above the Jordan Valley and the Dead Sea, from where, the Bible says, God showed Moses 'all the land of Gilead, unto Dan'. Moses died in Moab before the Israelites crossed the Jordan and according to the Bible was buried in a valley 'over against Beth-peor: but no man knoweth of his sepulchre unto this day'.

The remains of all the ancient Madabas lift the little modern town high enough above the dark red plain around it for it be seen from a long way off, like a mirage in the sky. It is now a market centre for some of the richest corn growing and sheep producing farmland in Jordan, so it seemed fitting that the Mayor on whom I called should be sitting at his desk on a cushion made from a thick woolly sheepskin.

Over coffee he explained that ever since ancient Biblical times, Madaba had been many things. It had once been a fine Roman city, full of temples and impressive public buildings, then a Christian city and the seat of a bishopric during which time many fine Byzantine mosaic floors were laid in the churches. The famous

79

map was one of them and if I cared to look, I could see many other wonderful mosaics, some dating back to Roman times, in what were now private houses.

The Mayor sent a young man to show me where these houses were, but first we stopped at the town's museum to see a fine mosaic paving which had recently been moved there after being discovered in use as a garage floor. It showed a man called Axia and over him a lion, representing his strength. Beside him was a friend playing a pipe, and in front of them, a woman, carrying a leafy branch, and dancing to the music. Over her head was a circlet held by two cherubs and round these figures scenes of the Golden Age represented by trees, sheep, gazelles, birds, another lion and a bull. It might have been the paving of a Roman villa, but the young man did not know, and the museum had not yet had the time to attach one of those useful explanation cards.

We walked down a narrow lane and into the courtyard of an old stone-built house. 'Look,' said my guide, pointing at the ground, but I could only see the faint outline of more mosaics until the man of the house came out, drew a bucket of water from a well in the corner and splashed it over the floor. Then suddenly a brilliant picture of birds, animals, and bunches of ripe grapes was there at my feet.

The owner invited us inside and showed us another lovely mosaic of a grey cockerel inside a scarlet cage. 'Perhaps it was meant to represent Christ in His prison,' he said. His wife took me into a bedroom and rolled back a carpet from the floor that was covering a mosaic of a lamb hanging on a tree – surely an early Christian representation of the Sacrifice – worked in still rich colours of golden yellow, blue, cream, grey and black. 'This house is built over what is believed must have been a fourth-century church,' she said, carefully replacing the carpet over the precious floor.

In another house I saw a mosaic of two sheep and a large, beautifully shaped urn, from which two peacocks were drinking. This mosaic had been discovered beneath the then existing floor of the house forty years ago by the grandfather of the present owner. This grandfather, my host told me, had come to Madaba from Karak at the end of the last century. So here was also the latest link in Madaba's checkered history, for in the 1880s a Christian community of about two thousand people had emigrated from Karak, once the great southern stronghold of the Crusaders in Palestine, and had settled in Madaba. They brought the town back to life, for gradually it had been abandoned, then left deserted for generations, after a disastrous earthquake in the eighth century.

Back in the bright sunshine, children were playing in the dusty lane and under their feet were probably more wonderful treasures waiting to be admired once again after centuries of oblivion. But much of Jordan is like this – a vast treasure house whose vaults have not yet been fully explored. Every time foundations are sunk for a new building, something of interest to the historian is found. A man has only to dig in his garden to turn up a reminder of his country's long and vivid past.

The Desert Patrol

'YOU'D BETTER TAKE two blankets each, it can be cold in the desert at night. I'll arrange for you to pick up a tent and a Land Rover at Guweira, the point where you will have to leave the Desert Highway and go into the desert itself, to get to Rumm.' My husband and I were planning a desert 'safari' to Petra, Wadi Rumm and Aqaba and were lucky to have the valuable help of Mr Ghaleb Barakat, head of Jordan's Tourism Authority. His department had just announced plans for building a branch road from the Highway across the Hasma desert into the Wadi Rumm, and setting up a camp there so that tourists could indulge in that most romantic of all adventures, a night in the silent desert under stars that loom large and bright as ten carat diamonds.

We had both read T E Lawrence's exciting description of Rumm as he, too, rode into the fabulous desert valley from Guweira during the Arab war against the Turks. And I had seen from a distance Rumm's great crimson-brown cliffs, wind-carved to shapes of wild fantasy and gilded by the desert sun, as I had travelled up and down the Desert Highway to Aqaba. One evening, at sunset, I had stopped my car at the best vantage point for Rumm, on the Highway, at Ras el Negeb, from where a high plateau four thousand feet above sea level dizzily plunges over two thousand feet to the desert below. There was a low mist over the reddening desert, hiding the bases of the sandstone cliffs of Rumm so that they seemed to be floating like sculptured islands on an opalescent sea. Even Petra, the 'rose-red city half as old as time', did not allure us as much as the thought of Rumm and a tent in the desert at the foot of its massive, painted mountains.

The Desert Highway runs straight as a Roman road for the two hundred and ten miles from Amman to Aqaba on the Red Sea. Part of it, in fact, runs over and alongside the ancient King's Highway of Old Testament days. This stretched from north of Damascus through the Amorites' stronghold of Rabbath Ammon (now Amman) on through the lands of the Moabites and Edomites east and south of the Dead Sea, through their capital of Selah, later known as Petra, and down to the tip of the deep valley now called the Wadi Arabah, at a point close to the present day site of modern Aqaba. From there, it branched west across the Sinai peninsular, to Egypt.

Abraham took the King's Highway north in victorious pursuit of the four kings who had captured his nephew Lot. Moses tried to lead the Exodus along it on the way out of the wilderness where they had wandered for forty years. 'Let us pass, I pray thee, through thy country,' Moses' messengers had said to the King of Edom. 'We will not pass through the fields or through the vineyards, neither will we drink of the water of the wells: we will go by the king's highway, we will not turn to the right hand nor to the left, until we have passed thy borders.' But the King said no and threatened to follow up his refusal with force, so Moses had to make a detour.

Fifteen hundred years later the Romans were still using the King's Highway. Parts of the paving which Trajan had laid along it, all the way from Damascus through Petra, to Aqaba, can still be seen.

The modern chariots that travel the Desert Highway are the great lorries that carry freight between Amman and Aqaba, Jordan's only port. Once a year they are joined by the Moslem pilgrims' buses festooned at night with strings of coloured fairy lights, and roaring their way down from Turkey and Syria through Jordan and the Hejaz desert in the south, towards Mecca.

The desert fortresses that used to guard the pilgrims' progress and provide safe stops for refreshment are no longer needed. Instead the buses and the lorries pull up at roadside cafés, and it

83

was in one of these we became involved in a drama. We talked so much to three Australian-bound young English travellers we met inside, that I left a cardigan behind. I did not miss it until I was back in the car and by the time I had returned to the café it had completely disappeared.

I could not believe it, for the Jordanians are honest. Dozens of times I have absent-mindedly left things behind all over the country and they have always been returned, or waiting for me when I went back. Within minutes a small crowd had appeared out of the desert night, all helping to search for the missing cardigan. Then by chance, a smart young police patrolman drove up on a motorcycle. A few words with the café owner, and he shot off up the road in the direction of Amman on the tail, someone explained, of a lorry driver and his mate who had been in the café while we were there.

I wanted to forget it and go on, but the café owner and his chums insisted we must stay. Twenty minutes later the policeman roared back, waving my cardigan aloft like a triumphant flag. A lorry trailed behind him.

The crowd beamed and clapped. I shook the policeman's hand and said thank you, we'll be off now, but he was a real 'Bobby' from the top of his white skidlid to the toes of his bright boots. He insisted we accompany him to the police headquarters at Ma'an, miles back up the road, so that he could make his report.

By now I was feeling sorry for the lorry driver who said he had picked up the cardigan, thinking it was his mate's. I believed him, but the policeman did not.

We followed the motorcycle in procession, our car, and the lorry, and pulled up in the courtyard outside a smartly painted and white-washed building. The policeman invited us to enter and when we did we felt as if we had walked on to a film-set by mistake. Round a table in a barely furnished office, a small group of men were playing cards. Three were in uniform, and were wearing revolvers, but the fourth and toughest looking of the lot was in striped pyjamas, his gun strapped round his middle.

He was the one who took command at once. Dignified and

stern, in spite of his pyjamas, he listened to the young policeman's story, looked us up and down with eyes that turned us inside out and stalked off into another room. Minutes later, he was back in an impeccably pressed khaki uniform, his revolver now strapped on to a Sam Browne, and we recognised his insignia as being those of a Major.

I had to identify my cardigan and tell how I had lost it. I added that now I had it back, couldn't we forget that it had been missing? But the Major too was a policeman to his fingertips. He listened to the explanations of the lorry driver and his mate, smiled grimly at the point where one was obviously trying to say that he thought the cardigan had belonged to his friend, and then waved the two men away.

'It cannot be forgotten. They are thieves and must be punished,' he said to me. 'Do they expect me to believe that one of them could wear this?' and he held my flimsy white cardigan up to the amusement of his colleagues who were still in the room and had been growling with indignant disbelief at the prisoners' story.

The two men were led outside into the night and the Major switched off his policeman look and became the charming Arab host. Coffee was brought in and as we talked we discovered that we would have met anyhow for it was the Major who had been asked to supply us with a Land Rover and driver to go to Rumm. The whole of the Desert Patrol south of Ma'an was under his command.

Just beyond Ma'an is Ras el Negeb, the spectacular edge of the plateau from where the Desert Highway begins a winding drop to a great plain of pink sand, two thousand feet below. Miles away, to the south-east, in the direction of the Saudi Arabian border are the *jebels* that lead into Wadi Rumm. The desert plain ahead slopes down eventually to Aqaba, Jordan's port and winter resort on the Red Sea.

From here on, the Hejaz railway, built by the Ottoman Turkish Sultan, Abd Al-Hamid, at the turn of this century to carry the Moslems from Damascus to Medina for the annual Haj pilgrimage to Mecca, and to provide quick transport south for the

Ottoman Empire's troops, was still a tangled ruin just as Colonel T E Lawrence and the Bedouin guerilla army of Emir Feisal had left it in 1918. An eight-million-pound-project of reconstruction had started only a few weeks before, and when the two British companies who won the contract have finished the job in 1967, the railway will once again connect Damascus with Medina, forty miles from the holy city of Mecca. Four hundred and fifty new bridges and thirty-eight new stations will have been built in the difficult five hundred miles stretch south from Ma'an.

We travelled fast over the plain until we came to Guweira, the camel market used by the Howeitat Bedouin, whose territory we were now in. More recently it has been developed as an army centre and a splendid new mosque rises above the tents and smart new bungalows. We stopped outside a double line of blanco-ed stones that marked the entrance to the guard room, where Major Abdullah had arranged for a Land Rover with a Desert Patrol driver to meet us.

Yasin, the driver, a private in the Police-force-cum-Army that is the Desert Patrol, introduced us to the engineer in charge of building a twenty-five mile stretch of new road that will lead from Guweira across the desert and into Rumm.

The morning was already hot and the drive across the plain had been dusty, so we were thankful for the glasses of mint tea the engineer produced for us in the shade of his tent. He was a former army major who had fought with the Allies in the Middle East in the last war, then against the Israelis at the end of the British Mandate. A Bedouin, he had all the desert man's respect and fierce loyalty for his King. 'Every day Hussein is getting more like his grandfather, Abdullah, whom I was proud to serve as a young man in the Army,' he said.

By the time we got back to the Land Rover we were amazed to see that two camp beds, complete with mattresses, had been loaded into the back. We had been prepared to sleep in our blankets on the sand. This was luxury.

Yasin and the two of us climbed up in front of the Land Rover and, in a cloud of dust and a flurry of cheerful hand waving from the engineer and his road gang, we were at last off across the desert to Rumm. For the first few miles we bumped along a firm but rocky surface, hitting the metal roof of the cabin occasionally as Yasin put his foot down to jump a dip. The desert was criss-crossed with heavy wheel tracks, made, Yasin told us, three years before by the supply trucks used by the film company which had shot some of the scenes for *Lawrence of Arabia* in Wadi Rumm.

Ahead we could see what looked like the shimmer of water, but Yasin said it was a *serab* (mirage), and as we reached it we saw that it was a *ghor* of sun-baked mud cracked by the heat of the summer into a million small crevices.

By now, my excitement at being so close to Wadi Rumm must have transmitted itself to Yasin for, laughing with glee like a schoolboy on holiday, he drove across the *ghor* as if it were a race-track.

After a couple of hair-raising miles we slowed down into soft sand and soon we were surrounded by the start of the two thous-and-feet-high *jebels* that form a glowing pink, gold and crimson wall on either side of a wide, sandy valley that is the beginning of Wadi Rumm. It was magnificent. All the pyramids in Egypt could be put inside this wadi and their vastness would diminish to the size of children's building blocks against a nursery wall.

Lawrence, who camped in Rumm with the Howeitat and their famous warrior Sheik Audeh Abu Tayih, described it in his book, *Seven Pillars of Wisdom,* as 'this processional way greater than imagination. The Arab armies would have been lost in the length and breadth of it and within the walls a squadron of aeroplanes could have wheeled in formation . . . landscapes in childhood's dream were so vast and silent.'

The twin watchtowers of a sandstone fortress which was so dwarfed by the *jebels* it looked like a toy in the distance came into sight. Soon we were sitting on the sand in front of it having coffee made over a brisk fire of dried tamarisk twigs and camel dung, by one of the Bedouin troops stationed at this most romantic of Desert Patrol outposts.

87

Our host was a handsomely moustachioed Sergeant, dressed like his troopers in a long khaki tunic and red and white checkered head-dress – the *keffiyeh* – held in place by two black cords – the *agal* – slanted at a rakish angle over one eye and decorated in the centre with the gold camel badge of the Corps. Two broad straps of brightly polished crimson leather crossed over his chest and glinted with brass bullets. In his crimson leather belt was a curved, silver handled dagger. A crimson, chiffon scarf fluttered from the gun holster on his hip. 'For cleaning your gun with?' I asked him. 'No, just for pretty,' he said, and roared with laughter at the joke.

The Sergeant and his men were part of the crack Camel Corps of the Desert Patrol which takes a foppish pride in its glamorous desert uniform, but is none the less tough and smartly disciplined for all that. In the forty years since the Corps was formed, by a British officer, Colonel F G Peake, these men have patrolled the Jordan desert on their camels to the point where it is now so law abiding anyone can travel in it with safety. Most of the troops and officers are Bedouin, picked for their intimate knowledge of the desert. Men recruited from the towns and villages would find it hard to understand the ways of the desert tribesmen and to keep up with their movements, but the Camel Corps always knows how best to keep the peace and exactly where to find a law-breaker when necessary.

After coffee, the Sergeant invited us inside the fortress to look at his office and the barrack rooms, then up a vertical wooden ladder to the roof, to watch the sun over the *jebels*. One of the men was leading a string of camels from the fortress to the foot of the *jebels* where the Sergeant told us there were springs with good supplies of fine water. Soon the camels were joined by a flock of goats from half a dozen black tents huddled together in the stretch of desert between the *jebels* and the fortress. The tents belonged to some men of the Howeitat who were helping to build the road from Guweira. The road had been started at both ends to speed the job up and was part of the Tourist Department's plans for building an overnight rest camp in the wadi.

By now, our tent had been put up and we decided to go over and unpack our picnic supper. But the Sergeant would not hear of it. 'Tonight you are our guests,' he said. 'Dinner will be ready soon.'

We walked across the sand, now glowing copper in the last light of the sun, and found the tent had been made wonderfully snug for us. The two camp beds were up and a strong wooden box had been upturned between them, for a table. There was fresh water in a bucket for washing, and drinking water in a bottle. There was also a sizeable audience of Bedouin waiting for us, who politely, but with intense fascination, watched us unpack. When we made a move to wash the western way, using the bucket as a sink, one of the men rushed forward and put us right.

In a pantomime which amused the audience no end, he asked us to hold out our hands and using an empty coffee tin, poured clean water over them as we rubbed away on the soap and rinsed our dusty faces. The men of the desert have a great respect for water. Using it the economical way, like this, what was left in the bucket was still clean and enough to last for a few more washings. Later we were told that the Arabs think our way of washing far less clean than theirs. They do not think much of the idea of washing their faces in the same water in which they have just washed their hands.

Someone brought in a hurricane lamp and hung it on the tent pole and we could see other flickers of light across the desert, where women were cooking the evening meal for their families outside their tents. The Sergeant and some of the men came over to talk to us and before long we were joined by a bearded young leader of the Howeitat, Sheik Jamil, and some of his friends. Soon, the tent was flowing over with visitors, some, like us, sitting on the beds, some on the floor and those who could not get inside making themselves comfortable round the entrance. Yasin, our happy-go-lucky driver, had disappeared. Later we were to find out why.

The Sergeant spoke enough English to act as interpreter for both sides, mostly learned, he told us, when he was in Scotland the year before for a Camel Corps display at the Edinburgh Tattoo. But if he had also picked up a Scots accent we could not detect it, maybe because the harsh, back-of-the-throat sounds in Arabic are practically the same as those a Scot will make when talking about lochs.

Our conversation was slow going, but hilarious at times, for the Arabs have a keen sense of humour which adds plenty of spice to their natural curiosity.

'How did you like Scotland?' we asked the Sergeant.

'Very much, but their camels were no good,' he said.

'Their camels?'

Our surprise was translated to the others and a great shout of laughter shook the tent. They had obviously heard that one before.

'Yes, they had two humps.'

Because of quarantine regulations, the Camel Corps had been forced to borrow camels from a zoo for their riding display and the only camels they could lay their hands on were the two-humped Bactrian kind. The Arabian camel of course has only one. The Sergeant took a long time to stop laughing at the memory of these 'Scottish' camels. He had picked up some hoary Scots jokes on the same trip and asked us if we had heard the one about the Scotsman who dropped a sixpence down a street grating and called out the fire brigade. The tent shook again.

Sooner or later we were bound to get on to the subject of age, and sure enough we did. It was the Sheik who started it. He asked the Sergeant to ask my husband how old I was. The Sergeant demurred a little, but the Sheik insisted. My husband gallantly said I had better speak for myself, so I ventured, 'Twenty-one'.

The Sheik leaned a little closer and took as good a look as the light from the hurricane lamp allowed, then in polite disbelief jerked up his chin – the Arab equivalent of shaking one's head, and said '*La*' – no!

This was counted as a joke too, and even I had a good laugh. But the Sheik would not give up. 'I have,' he said to my husband, 'four wives. How many have you?'

'One, and that is I,' I said, getting the answer in first.

The Sheik then came in for a great deal of good natured teasing about his four wives. He must be very rich, and strong, to manage to keep four, he was told, it was bad enough having one . . . but although with his count of four he topped the list of those present, he was not the only one among us with more than one wife. The Sergeant told us he had two, and nine children, but he was happy to say they all got on well together. We all congratulated the happy Sergeant – 'mabruk, mabruk' – congratulations. He beamed with pleasure and at that point a delicious meaty smell filled the tent and in staggered Yasin and one of the Bedouin carrying between them a dish the size of a coffee table, piled high with steaming rice and meat.

Dinner was ready, and Yasin had spent the last two hours cooking it. A sheep had been killed to make a traditional Bedouin *mensaf* for us. The hospitality of our hosts was never-ending. The meat had been boiled with herbs then torn into large pieces and carefully arranged over the enormous mound of rice. Right on top was the head, without, we were relieved to notice, the eyes. That custom, it seems, is a Syrian one anyway. But everything else was there.

The talk stopped abruptly. The Bedouin do not believe in mixing the serious business of eating with chatter. All those who could manage it crowded round the dish and then for us came the problem. No spoons or forks. We hung back a bit to see what the form was. Everybody else dug in with their hands, skilfully pulling off bits of meat and scooping up the rice.

We tried the meat, and it was almost too hot to handle but it tasted good. The Sheik and the Sergeant as main hosts selected special titbits of meat for us and dropped them in front of our places round the dish. The brains were scooped out of the sheep's skull and given to me. My husband got the delicacies always reserved for the male guest of honour. Each time Yasin felt the food was getting too cool he scooped up a ladleful of boiling stock and poured it over the dish.

By sticking to the meat we were managing quite well. But the rice was tricky until the Sheik showed us how. He took a small amount and rolled it in his palm until it formed a ball, then with a flick of the wrist popped it into his mouth. After one or two messy attempts we could manage that too, and what beautifully cooked rice it was. Soft, but still slightly nutty, as boiled rice should be but hardly ever is. Obviously Yasin had not bothered to fiddle about with strainers and steamers to get it perfect either. He must have been a born cook. More shouts of '*mabruk*' and this time it was Yasin who was beaming proudly.

As we, the first wave of diners, slowed down and retired, a second wave moved in and then a third until the enormous plate was clean. One by one our visitors said goodnight and went out into the desert to their own tents or the fortress. The Bedouin like to have their evening talk before the meal, not afterwards, as we do. Once the food – the climax of the evening – is finished, they thank the host and get up and go.

We took a short stroll outside too, before turning in and watched a full moon rise straight between the black silhouette of a cleft in the *jebels*. As it came up it shone on the tops of the crags until they seemed to be running with quick-silver. Half an hour later the whole wadi was flooded with moonlight and the mighty *jebels* and tiny fortress looked as if they had been cut out of stiff black paper, like the scenery in a Chinese shadow play.

We woke about 5.30, feeling wonderfully fresh. Getting up at home at such a time in the morning would normally turn me into a semi-conscious sleepwalker for the first couple of hours, but the night of the desert in summer is cool and exhilarating and, until the sun gets hot, makes you feel you can conquer the world. The moment my husband opened the tent flaps one of our *mensaf* friends rushed up with two glasses of sweet, scalding hot tea. Everybody had been up and about long before us.

We wandered across to the fortress to say goodbye and thank you to the Sergeant and his men and ask if we might take some photographs. 'Of course, but first some coffee,' they said. Their camels were already saddled for patrol with gay red- and black-woven Bedouin shawls edged with tassels beneath their saddles and tasselled saddle bags on either side.

'They and we were photographed many times while the film *Lawrence* was being made here,' the Sergeant told us. 'We all took part in it.' And like well-trained film stars, the camels turned their haughty profiles to our camera as soon as we produced it.

'Would you like to ride one?' the Sergeant asked me. It was too good an opportunity to miss, even though I had no idea how to get on or off. He made his camel kneel and helped me into the saddle showing me how to sit in the riding position with one foot tucked under the knee of the other leg, then how to lean away as the camel tipped forward to unfold its lanky back legs, and smartly lean forwards as it rocked up into a standing position. I clung to the high pommel for the ground below might have been soft sand but it was quite a long way down. '*Hut, hut,*' the Sergeant said to his camel, and it loped off across the desert giving the Wadi Rumm Camel Corps their first laugh of the day.

Reluctantly we had to leave, for we had an early morning coffee date at the tent of Sheik Jamil, and were going on to Petra. The Sheik's tent was a few miles further up the wadi where the pink-flowered, feathery-leaved tamarisk and grey-green camel thorn was thick. He had invited his father-in-law, another sheik, to meet us and they were waiting with some of their men by Jamil's tent.

The front of the tent was wide open to the sun and a brightly coloured rug was spread on the sand, with cushions for us to lean on. One of Jamil's men roasted the coffee beans in a long-handled spoon over the fire, pounded them in a mortar and soon we were sipping the strong, black Bedouin coffee that he poured in a ceremoniously high stream into the cups from a heavy brass pot.

The cushion on which I was propping myself up with one elbow was beautifully embroidered with tiny red, green, black and white glass beads and I recognised the pattern as being the Jordanian flag. 'Made by my daughter, his wife,' the elder Sheik said. Whatever position she might have held in the young Sheik's household, and we did not like to ask, this wife was at least a talented needlewoman.

'If she is here, can I meet her?' I asked the two Sheiks, and the father pointed to behind another rug which was hanging to one side of the tent as a dividing curtain, to provide a room for the women.

I got up and walked round to the back of it, and a pretty young girl stood facing me. She shyly shook my hand, but after answering her welcome my scanty Arabic dried up, so we just kept on smiling at one another. I wanted to give her a present, but the only thing I had was a silk scarf printed with South Sea island palms and hula girls, a cruise souvenir. But she seemed delighted.

As I went back to my place on the coffee carpet, she must have whispered the news to her husband from her side of the rug, for none of the men could have seen us together. He immediately leaned forward and pulled the beaded cover off the cushion, folded it and asked me to accept it from his wife.

My husband, who had no idea what was going on, looked hard at me, but I could not explain until we got back to the Land Rover. I felt a little shattered too, for until then I had forgotten the strict code of the Bedouin in always making a gift in return. The Sheik's young wife must have spent many hours embroidering the cushion cover which is now a treasured reminder of our 'safari' to Wadi Rumm. And I have often wondered since what she made of the hula girls.

The Rose-Red City

THE REST HOUSE is built into a rocky hill, pitted with caves, about a mile outside Petra. It was in one of these caves that the Swiss explorer, Burkhardt, camped before riding on down the valley to be the first European for six hundred years to enter the deserted, ancient city which had been lost to the outside world since the time of the Crusades.

Camel caravans carrying frankincense, myrrh, spices and gold from Southern Arabia two thousand years and more ago when Petra was the splendid capital of a kingdom which stretched as far north as Damascus, probably halted at these caves instead of going inside the city. Later, when Petra and its Nabatean kingdom became a province of Rome, the caves might have been used as a police post and stables for the horses of the Imperial Roman Army. But now they have been turned into a dining room for the rest house and the travellers using them are tourists from all over the world, lured to this place by the fascination of the 'rose-red city, half as old as time'.

Until 1963, when the rest house was opened, you either visited Petra in one rugged day, setting off from Amman one hundred and sixty-nine miles away, at five in the morning and getting back in time for a late dinner, or spent the night at the rest camp which an enterprising Amman hotelier has built among the ruins of the old city. If you were lucky you managed to get one of the few rooms inside the camp's main building, or a tent. If you were not, or a romantic, depending on how you look at things, you slept inside one of the many caves that the Nabateans had used as houses or tombs, and latterly the Bedouin had used as winter quarters.

The caves, which are still being used as bedrooms, are sparsely furnished, but clean, and have running water. I have never tried sleeping in one. I find Petra brooding and sinister enough by day when the desert sun fills it with golden light. At night, it must be overwhelming. But whatever you might feel about this city of the dead which was carved into the great sandstone rocks that hide it completely from the outside world, you will not be disappointed.

It is not unique. Two hundred miles south in the Hejaz desert of Saudi Arabia there is another deserted city, Meda'in Salih, which was also carved out of the rock by the Nabateans, the nomadic tribe who came down from what is now Jordan in the sixth century BC and overran the land of the Biblical Edomites. But there is no other entrance to any city in the world that is as dramatic as the road into Petra.

Even from the new rest house, where you get on the horse that will take you the last mile down the rocky mountain path into the city, all you can see in front of you is a jagged line of seemingly impassable sandstone crags. The clack of hooves and the shouts of the Arab boys who are leading the horses start to echo as the path narrows into a towering natural cleft in the crags. This is the famous Siq, the only way in and Petra's impregnable defence for centuries. A handful of men could hold this entrance against an army, and did so many times.

In places the rocky walls almost meet overhead and the wild figs and bright pink oleanders growing in the cracks have to struggle for the sun. You can still see the channel cut into the foot of the rocks that used to carry water to the cisterns and public baths of Petra from the abundant spring of Ain Musa, one of the traditional spots where Moses struck rock and water gushed forth.

Ain Musa is now two miles behind you, basking in the hot sun that you are already missing after a few minutes inside this chill, gloomy tunnel which winds so much it is impossible to see the path ahead for more than a few yards. Then suddenly it is over. The rock opens out like the mouth of a cavern and framed outside in the sunlight is a vast temple façade, carved in perfect proportion into the soft sandstone face of a mountain.

(above) *Winifred Carr meets the King in the Basman Palace.* (below) *The marriage ceremony performed at the Zahran Palace by a sheik of the Moslem Sharia Court. In the background are Sherif Hussein bin Nasser* (left), *the King's uncle, and Hussein's Chief Aide-de-camp*

(*above, left*) *The King's office in the Basman Palace, overlooked by a portrait of his grandfather, King Abdullah. Two Circassians of the Royal Bodyguard are in attendance.* (*right*) *An exterior view of the Basman Palace*

The Raghadan Palace, Amman

It is obviously no accident that this temple, El Khaznah, is the most impressive of all the monuments in Petra. Whoever made the decision to have it carved here must first have carefully studied the breathtaking effect it would have on anyone coming out of the gloom of the Siq. From outside it looks like a two-storied building faced with pedimented pillars, its entrance a great doorway, forty feet high. But inside it is surprisingly small. There is one empty, unadorned room with three smaller rooms leading off. It is rather like finding a large and flashy shopwindow fronting a little one-man kiosk.

Two hundred feet up, above the doorway, a stone urn is balanced on top of the carvings. Generations of Bedouin and travellers have pitted its surface with gunshot because of a tradition that it is full of treasure. But archaeologists have discovered that this too, like the rest of the building, is carved out of solid rock.

Nobody knows exactly what El Khaznah was built for – temple or tomb – although the experts think it was more likely used as a temple than anything else. But the most mysterious thing about the place, for me at least, is the inscription in firm black lettering on one of the inside walls of five very British sounding names and the date 1836. 'Charlotte Rowley, R Rowley, H Ker Seymer, W Cudway, H Moore.' These names inspire visions of a long and hazardous trek across the desert at the mercy of guides who might turn out to be treacherous, by four intrepid Englishmen and the wife or sister of one of them who probably had to ride side-saddle all the way because of her crinoline. It was only twenty-two years before that Burkhardt had rediscovered Petra, but this adventurous vanguard of the thousands of tourists to come had braved formidable dangers to see the long lost city for themselves.

Even forty years ago it was a difficult enough trip to make. The people living in Wadi Musa and the Bedouin who camped in and around Petra during the winter months disliked strangers to the point of murdering the first men stationed at the small mud-walled fortress that is the police patrol post in the village of Elji.

From El Khaznah you ride on past more tombs and temples

G   97 until you come to the Roman amphitheatre which once seated three thousand people and then the rocky path stretches into the remains of a paved street edged with the bases of what once must have been splendid columns. The rest camp is at the end of this street, and from then on, if you want to see more, you have to climb.

Perhaps at the right time of day, when the sun is setting and at its reddest, this deserted city of carved rocks does turn rose-red. But mostly the carved buildings are copper coloured and gold or a soft lilac with blue-grey streaks. In places where they have been weathered by sandstorms and desert winds they look like vast edifices of raspberry, vanilla and blackcurrant ice-cream, melting in the desert sun.

The Jordan Department of Antiquities is clearing and restoring the lovely amphitheatre and some enterprising Jordanians have dreams of turning it into the world's most dramatic site for moonlight drama festivals. But it is not a practical dream. An audience of three thousand could hardly be put up for the night there, and they would have to be, or face a three-hour drive back to Amman after the performance. And a modern road would have to be built through the Siq. The Department of Antiquities is against that, for it feels cars and coaches pouring into Petra would ruin the peaceful secretive atmosphere, and they are right.

When the spring and summer tourist season is over, Petra sinks back into the silence it has known since the camel caravans began to bypass it and its prosperous trade was snatched by the rival city of Palmyra, in the north. Then the only regular visitors still passing through the Siq are the members of the Commonwealth Save The Children Fund who work among the Bedouin south of Ma'an. They have turned one of the caves near the rest camp into a feeding centre and clinic for the children of the Bedouin tribe that lives in this city of the dead.

The Fund's brown-and-cream jeep was standing outside the centre on the morning we rode into the camp and the wooden door to the cave was wide open. Inside, one of the medical assistants, a young Arab, was setting out the food supplies for the week.

The menus are planned by a dietician and provide the children who regularly visit the centre with most of the square meals they are likely to have. Generally the food is of the sort their mothers would serve if they could afford to – meat stew with lentils or rice, *burghul* which is a nourishing dish of boiled, cracked wheat, *hummus*, a thick paste made from boiled chickpeas and seseme oil, flavoured with garlic, lemon and salt, which is scooped up with pieces of bread, and the thick, creamy yoghurt the Arabs call *laban*. Sardines, tinned soup, corned beef, skimmed milk, soya flour, sugar and vitamin tablets are included in the menus and although the Bedouin children might find them strange additions at first, they seem to be thriving on them.

'Once a fortnight a doctor attends the clinic and now that there is a school, too, the children here are beginning to catch up with those who have an easier life in the towns and villages,' the assistant told us.

A school in Petra, the first one for thirteen hundred years, was worth taking a look at, but we could see no sign of it. 'It's about five minutes' walk away, over those rocks, and down towards the wadi bed,' we were told. 'When one of the boys comes in, I'll ask him to show you.' So we sat for a while and talked to the young man and his elder brother who was visiting him. The brother had emigrated to the United States some years before and was making his first trip back to Jordan, full of the advantages of living in Detroit, but proud to show his teenage daughters the country he still called home.

Later we walked down to the school and found a small square concrete building dwarfed by the rocks which hid it from the main road and the camp. The young Arab teacher lives in one of its two rooms and teaches twenty-two boys aged from five to fifteen in the other, taking each group for ten minutes at a time. He told us the boys were so keen to learn that the start of the new term is a greater treat for them than the start of the holiday. At the moment there are no facilities for opening a class for girls, but some of what the boys are learning is rubbing off on their sisters and parents.

99

'A wonderful thing happened here yesterday,' the teacher said. 'We found water in the wadi bed and the boys' fathers are digging a well. Come and see.'

A group of men, ankle deep in muddy water, were digging happily a few yards away from the building. The water had been located by one of the technical assistants from the Department of Antiquities team working in Petra. Until this discovery the teacher and his boys had to fetch the school's water supplies from a mile away, and until the classroom was built the nearest school was nearly two hours' donkey ride away. So all round, life was getting a little easier for these young Bedouin children.

A doctor's clinic, a school and a regular supply of sweet water are the three things that are tempting many of Jordan's two hundred and twenty thousand Bedouin away from their traditional home on the steppe and in the desert. Those who find it impossible to settle in the towns or farming villages are being drawn to small settlements of houses that the Government is building as the Central Water Authority provides more wells, south of Ma'an and east of the Desert Highway to Aqaba.

This programme of resettlement was initiated by King Hussein who takes a close personal interest in the welfare of Bedouin tribesmen. For thousands of years these nomadic tribesmen, who believe only they have the right to be called Arab, a name meaning people of noble blood and tent dwellers, have been constantly on the move, looking for fresh grazing for their camels, sheep and goats, but always on a fixed itinerary and within their own tribal territories. The name Bedouin comes from the Arabic *Al Bedou* which means inhabitant of the desert, and strictly speaking only applies to the camel herding tribes who traditionally were the aristocrats of the nomads. They ranged further than the others, constantly travelling between Syria and Saudi Arabia, and forced many of the weaker tribes, the sheep and goat herders, to pay them tribute, until the Government stamped out the practice.

The *ghazu*, the tribal raids for loot or vengeance, have also been eliminated by the Desert Patrol, the Government police force of the desert. The last one took place over thirty years ago.

In the spring, after the winter rains, the steppe and the desert in Jordan are green with plenty of grazing, and the tribes might stay in one place for weeks, until the drier months force them to move on seeking areas where the desert shrubs have retained moisture and nutrition and there is another waterhole. During the driest months of the summer the Bedouin tend to move towards the settled areas to trade milk, yoghurt, butter and cheese from their herds, and carpets woven from the hair of their camels, sheep and goats by the women.

King Hussein, who is a member of the Qoreish tribe of the Hejaz, into which the Prophet Mohammed was born and many of the caliphs and kings who succeeded him, is strongly supported by the Bedouin. The Hashemite dynasty, to which the King belongs, is descended from the Prophet's daughter Fatima and for generations was the traditional guardian of Mecca. So the Bedouin owe Hussein a double allegiance. He is the religious head of their tribes as well as their King and for those Bedouin who form the bulk of Jordan's Army, he also has a special place in their affection as their Commander-in-Chief.

As often as he can the King goes into the desert to spend a few days among the black tents and many times he has said these are among the happiest days of his life. He gets impatient sometimes with the stuffiness of court protocol and likes the informality of the desert where although he is religious leader, King and Commander-in-Chief, he is plain 'Hussein' to the Bedouin. A man's honour, courage and hospitality are the things that count among the Bedouin, and King Hussein has shown to the world as well as his own people that he has plenty of all three.

He enjoys riding with the tribesmen, joining in their traditional dances and songs and sitting talking with them in the coffee tent. He is always ready to listen to even the poorest tribesmen's petitions and tries to deal with their problems on the spot. As their Sheik of Sheiks, he is the man the tribesmen feel they must ask direct, whenever there is anything they need.

King Hussein has said that he hopes in the not too distant future most of the Bedouin will be permanently settled on the land given to them by the Government and there are some who predict that within fifty years their ancient nomadic way of life will be finished in Jordan.

To us who live in comfort, able to get water at the turn of a tap, send our children to school and eat three square meals a day without going to much trouble, life in the desert has a rosy glow of romance and freedom. But the desert is the most merciless place on earth, a cruel land where it is a hard struggle for man to keep himself and his family alive. Nobody knows this better than the Bedouin.

Aqaba on the Red Sea

UNTIL 1965 JORDAN's only outlet to the sea funnelled into
five miles of coastline at the tip of the Gulf of Aqaba, one of the
twin horns at the head of the Red Sea. Then a further eleven miles
of coastline to the south-east was conceded to Jordan by Saudi
Arabia. For many centuries before the Arab-Jewish war, Haifa
and Jaffa on the Mediterranean coast were the main ports for the
Arabs of Palestine and Transjordan. Aqaba was a slumbering little
fishing village with only memories of having been important and
prosperous in Biblical days as the port where gold, silver, ivory,
apes and peacocks from 'distant Ophir' were unloaded and
frankincense and myrrh from Southern Arabia.

The road that the Romans built from Damascus through Petra
branched off west at Aqaba and linked up with the ancient military and trade route across the Sinai peninsular, to Egypt. From
Petra to Aqaba now takes less than two hours to drive and we
followed part of the way of the Roman road south to the Red Sea,
through the land of the Biblical Edomites who were said to be the
descendants of Esau. Perhaps it was somewhere along this way
that the hungry tribesman sold his birthright to his crafty brother
Jacob for a pottage of goat's meat.

On the Desert Highway just outside Aqaba a military post was
a reminder that we were back on the edge of no man's land. In
front of us was the brand new town of Aqaba that by 1968 will
have replaced the old fishing village entirely. A little to the right,
on the same curve of the head of the Gulf but across the armistice
line we could see another brand new port and town, Eilat. Sitting

beneath the palms on Aqaba's beach you can look left into the Saudi Arabian desert and right into Israeli and Egyptian territory all in the sweep of twenty miles, for the four countries meet on this narrow, politically vital arm of the Red Sea.

Jordanian and Israeli port police patrol their own stretches of the Gulf. Ships sail out of Aqaba and can freely turn right, into the Suez Canal – unlike the ships leaving Eilat. But holiday-makers, with casual disregard for political tension, laze on the beach at Aqaba and just as comfortably explore the magnificent coral reefs off-shore in glass-bottomed boats. The more energetic fish, swim, skin-dive and water-ski in the always warm and crystal-clear sea.

If you happen to be there on a Friday it is more than likely that you will see King Hussein tirelessly and expertly ski-ing around the bay, as he was this particular Friday morning. An international water-ski rally was planned for the following week and the King, who was to lead a team from Jordan, was practising manœuvres. Whenever he can he sets off from Amman on Thursday afternoons and drives his family down the Desert Highway to reach their bungalow on the beach at Aqaba in time for dinner. He can relax here with his wife, who is also an expert water-skier, and their children, away from court protocol and his office. And at the same time he can watch the development of Aqaba into Jordan's newest town, winter resort and one of the Middle East's busiest ports, a project that is close to his heart.

The King has favoured the plan right from the start, realising that Jordan could hardly prosper without her own seaport and has encouraged and followed every step of its rapid growth from drawing board to reality. So much is Aqaba Hussein's 'own' that even the holiday bungalow he has had built there was his personal project, just as the new house at Hummar was Princess Muna's. There was some friendly family rivalry about the two houses which were built at the same time. 'Planning Hummar was my particular project,' Princess Muna has told me. 'Planning the house at Aqaba was His Majesty's and although mine was started about eighteen months before his it became a race towards the end as to which would be ready first. Hummar won, but only by a few weeks.'

But then, there is a bustling atmosphere in Aqaba that seems to infect everything. It was only two years before this visit that I had first been there, yet I could hardly recognise the place now. The crumbling, twelfth-century stone fortress was still there. So was the mud palace right at the water's edge that Lawrence and Sheik Audeh Abu Tayih of the Howeitat had used as their head-quarters after capturing Aqaba from the Turks in 1917. The palace was still being used, as it had been on my first visit, as offices by the Governor of Aqaba and the Police until the new civic build-ings were ready. But the cluster of little open-fronted shops that had been the colourful market of the town had almost disappeared to make room for a new commercial centre. And on the beach among the palms a gleaming white holiday hotel with its own colony of self-contained beach cabanas had been built. The port was busier than I remembered it. A new wharf had been added to the dock area and sites were being levelled for civic buildings, schools, a college and houses.

By the time the new town is finished, forty thousand people will be living there in homes that will all have a sea view, thanks to clever planning. Those on the front will be bungalows, the first row behind will be single-storied and the second row double-storied, and no one will be allowed to deviate from this. Broad, palm tree-shaded avenues will lead to the new commercial centre which will be built around a large public square. The small air-field on which King Hussein lands when he comes down by plane will be turned into a modern airport, so that Aqaba will be con-nected with Amman and Jerusalem by regular flights. A boule-vard will lead from it, bypassing the town centre to join up with a seaside drive leading to the beach, a new yachting harbour, an aquarium, sports stadium, tropical gardens and the docks.

A mosque, its minaret towering as high as a lighthouse, was the first new building to go up and the empty plot alongside it was still being used as a temporary parking area for the fleet of heavy trucks that carry most of Jordan's imports fifty-two miles up the Desert Highway to Ras el Negeb, the present head of the Hejaz railway. From there the cargoes are sent by rail across the rolling

105

stony desert to Amman and Jerusalem two hundred miles and more north. On their return to Ras el Negeb the trains bring potash and phosphates for export from Aqaba, but once the railway has been extended they will be able to steam right into the dock area.

So once again Aqaba is an important sea gate for trade between the Middle East and the rest of the world, as archaeologists have discovered it was in the time of King Solomon three thousand years ago.

The actual site of Solomon's ship building port of Ezion Geber probably lies under a low mound, Tell al Khalaifah, which is now nearly a mile away from the sea and almost on the armistice line. When it was possible to excavate there, the remains of an ancient city and copper smelting furnaces and casting moulds were found. The site had been cleverly placed at the head of the Wadi Arabah, the great cleft in the land that runs down from the Dead Sea to Aqaba and which is a natural wind tunnel. The winds that constantly blow down the wadi were skilfully channelled through a system of air passages so that they could be used for smelting the copper brought from Solomon's copper mines in the wadi's hills.

Apparently the copper works were abandoned some time in the fifth century BC and the port was moved two miles east to the site of present-day Aqaba, comfortably out of the path of the winds coming down the wadi. As the new town of Aqaba goes up, fragments of glass, pottery and carved stone are constantly being found on the building sites, proof that the place must have had extensive trade with South Arabia and continued to flourish for nearly a thousand years more, until the beginning of Islam in the seventh century.

It was still strategically important enough at the beginning of the twelfth century for the Crusaders to fight for it. During the time they occupied the town they built a fortress which still stands offshore. Later on Aqaba became one of the gateways to Mecca for pilgrims who preferred to travel by sea to Jeddah instead of joining the Haj caravans that went overland through the Hejaz Desert. It still is a landing place for travellers coming up from the

Saudi Arabian port and from Aden, who prefer to go by sea rather than fly or drive.

Our drive down from Petra had been hot and dusty, so first we swam, then we walked along the beach to look at the exotic shells and branches of coral that the fishermen spread out for sale under the palms. When the coral is first brought out of the sea it is delicately tinted in a dozen different colours and the piece we bought was pale lilac, shaped like a Victorian posy and still damp. A few days later after being left out in the hot sun to dry and lose its overpoweringly fishy smell, it had bleached bone white. It was a pity about the colour, but at least we could then live in the same room as it.

The fish taken out of the Red Sea at Aqaba are no less exotic than the shells and coral and most of them are delicious, particularly one that has the same flaky texture and delicate flavour of salmon, but is chocolate brown instead of pink when cooked.

During the summer months Aqaba can be one of the hottest places in Jordan and the air conditioning in the new buildings will have to be kept working overtime. But from October to March the climate is perfect for beaching and bathing. Once the regular flights to Aqaba begin, a few days on this lovely palm fringed tropical beach will round off most people's winter holiday in the Holy Land, particularly at Christmas time when Jerusalem, Bethlehem and the Judean hills might be glittering under a dusting of frost.

107

Castles in the Desert

THERE IS A sort of desert daftness that the English are particularly prone to – think of Lawrence, Gertrude Bell, Lady Hester Stanhope, Sir Richard Burton and particularly Charles Doughty, the Victorian scholar and explorer who spent two years, mainly in persecuted misery and constant danger to his life, roaming that part of the Arabian desert that is now in Saudi Arabia. This romantic craving for the cruelly burning, wide open spaces is something that the Bedouin, who dream of cool, green gardens and splashing water, consider quite crazy.

At Wadi Rumm we caught it. By the time we got back to Amman we had only one day left of our holiday, and we planned to spend it in the Black Desert, north and east of the capital, seeing as many of the old desert castles as we could.

These castles were built as hunting lodges by those men of the southern desert, the Omayyad Caliphs, in the eighth century. Damascus, a thousand miles away from their native Hejaz, was their capital, but in the summer the city hemmed them in too much so they escaped to the desert that surrounds that great oasis. Their days were spent hunting gazelles, hares, wild partridge and the tawny Asian lion, with hawks and cheetahs, and their nights around the coffee fires outside their tents.

Eventually they built delightful little hunting lodges, some starkly utilitarian, others luxurious pleasure palaces exquisitely decorated with painted frescoes, marble paving, ornamental pools and mosaic-lined steam baths where they could while away the summer in splendid comfort when not out following the chase on their beautiful Arabian horses.

A few of the castles were built on the crumbling remains of Roman outpost fortresses. The more sumptuous ones were the graceful designs of Persian and Byzantine architects. Their ruins dot the Syrian and Jordanian desert and the best of them are roughly east of a line between Amman and Madaba. Apart from Khirbet al Mafjar, Caliph Hisham's palace near Jericho, and Mushetta, about an hour's drive out of Amman, these castles are deep in the desert that rolls east from the Hejaz railway towards the Saudi Arabian border.

To get to them you need a tough car and an even tougher driver who must know his way and, even then, preferably carry a compass. There are no maps, signposts or roads, only a confusion of crossed tracks in some places which suddenly appear and seem to go nowhere, and in other places nothing at all to indicate to the inexperienced eye which way to turn. Try driving across this desert on your own and you might wander around in circles until found by the Bedouin or the Desert Patrol. Be prepared to get smothered from head to foot in dust too, for the car will whip up what feels like half the desert. And if you are planning to take photographs this is one trip on which you will really need a lens brush.

Warned about all the snags by our friends in Amman, then generously supplied with another Land Rover and an excellent driver, Ahmed, who had visited the desert castles many times, we packed a picnic and bottles of water and set off soon after dawn. After a short diversion for coffee at Ahmed's house on the outskirts of town, we headed first for Zerka.

Passing the Army camp that is the focal point of the town, Ahmed suddenly left the road, and we were in the desert. For a while, there were people; supply trucks thundering towards the camp, a small village, a tent, then nothing but dusty, stony ground, a few struggling patches of scrub and shimmering flats of salt-crusted land ahead that looked so much like lakes we fancied we could see the reflections of trees in them. When at last we were sure there was a real oasis with real palm trees ahead, neither dared mention it, in case we were fooled again. But this time it was true. 'Azraq,' said Ahmed.

Palaeolithic hand-axes two hundred thousand years old have been found in this oasis, which is a lush series of palm-fringed lakes and pools. The Romans built a fortress there of black basalt, for this is where the black desert of basalt and lava begins, spreading from the outskirts of the oasis up into Syria and east towards Saudi Arabia. Flying over it, as I later did, it looks like a grim, dark sea swelling in waves on to a golden beach that is the desert we had just driven across from Zerka.

The Roman fortress which guarded the northern end of an ancient caravan highway was repaired and used centuries later by the Arabs and was known to the Crusaders. Then, like that other desert stronghold, Petra, it seems to have been 'lost' for centuries until the Army of the Arab Revolt and Lawrence used it as headquarters from which to harry the Turks in the north.

In the *Seven Pillars of Wisdom,* Lawrence wrote, 'It was to be Ali's first view of Azraq, and we hurried up the stony ridge in high excitement, talking of the wars and songs and passions of the early shepherd kings, with names like music, who had loved this place; and of the Roman legionaires who languished here as garrison in yet earlier times. Then the blue fort on its rock above the rustling palms, with the fresh meadows and shining springs of water, broke on our sight. Of Azraq, as of Rumm, one said *"Numen inest"*. Both were magically haunted : but where Rumm was vast and echoing and God-like, Azraq's unfathomable silence was steeped in knowledge of wandering poets, champions, lost kingdoms, all the crime and chivalry and dead magnificence of Hira and Ghassan. Each stone or blade of it was radiant with half-memory of the luminous silky Eden, which had passed it so long ago.'

Lawrence had lived in the room above the southern gate tower of the castle and we climbed up to see it. An arched window opened on to the inner courtyard and the three other windows in the thick walls were nothing more than defence slits for shooting through when necessary. There was a fireplace, but no chimney. Lawrence must have been kippered with smoke when a fire was lit.

Dark and draughty, with less light coming from the windows in the walls than from the cracks between the stone beams of the roof through which the rain used to drip on to Lawrence's coffee fire, we felt it was no wonder that he and his Bedouin used to hear the legendary dogs of the ancient builders of the fortress howling around the towers at night in search of their dead masters. 'At such times our men pounded the coffee harder while the Arabs broke into sudden song to occupy their ears against the misfortune. No Bedouin would lie in wait for the mystery, and from our windows we saw nothing but the motes of water in the dank air which drove through the radiance of our firelight. So it remained a legend; but wolves or jackals, hyenas, or hunting dogs, their ghost watch kept our ward more closely than arms could have done,' he wrote. Myth or not, the thought of the ghostly dogs soon drove me out of Lawrence's dark room and into the bright sunshine.

Guarding the oasis today is another of those romantic looking little desert forts of the Camel Corps. We reported our arrival and intended journey to the corporal at the gate and were invited in for coffee. There we met a young man who told us he was a customs officer, which started thoughts of smugglers' caravans riding through the desert at night with contraband stuffed in their camel bags. But it was nothing like that he was there to keep an eye on. He explained that the salt pans around the oasis were being worked and there was a tax of one fils, about a farthing, on each kilo. He invited us across to his office for more coffee, told us he was studying for a university degree in his spare time, of which he had plenty in this lonely place, and he begged us to stay as long as we could and 'just talk'.

Full of coffee and talking too much, we did not notice the time until Ahmed broke the party up by indicating it was now midday and we ought to picnic before moving on. We sought out a quiet spot beneath the palms by one of the pools and while we ate watched two small boys having a glorious time floating around

111

on an old truck tyre. Ahmed looked at his watch again. 'Let's go on. If we set off now we should be able to see Amra, Kharanah and Mushetta before dark. It's about another hundred kilometres, even if we don't get lost.'

We bumped and jolted across miles of flinty wilderness, seeing no landmarks by which Ahmed could be finding his way other than a few bleak tamarisk bushes. But he just pressed on until suddenly there was something new ahead, a low stone building with a triple-arched roof, and a black tent pitched beside it. 'Qasr Amra,' Ahmed said, wiping a thick layer of dust off his face and looking rather like Columbus must have done at landfall.

Broken pieces of polished white marble were scattered about the ground outside the little castle and we could see traces of plaster still clinging to the walls. A large well-head lined with curved blocks of stone still had water somewhere deep down inside it. We heard it splash as we dropped a stone over the edge, but could not see it. This well had once supplied the water for the Caliph's luxurious bath which was complete with furnace room, calidarium, where he could practically boil, and a frigidarium.

The triple-arched roof covered three small vaulted halls, built side by side. Inside them it was blissfully cool but so dark we could only see the outlines of the walls and ceilings. The one thing we had not thought of bringing was a torch. Ahmed made our misery at realising our mistake more intense by telling us that the walls of these vaulted halls were frescoed with wonderful paintings, and so were the ceilings of the bath rooms. We struck match after match, but saw only faint tracings of painted plaster on the crumbling surfaces.

'Never mind, you will come again, insh'Allah,' Ahmed said with the soothing philosophy of the true Arab. 'Insh'Allah' – if God wills – we echoed. As we climbed back into the Land Rover a Bedouin came out of the tent alongside the castle and came across to us. After the usual prolonged greetings of the desert had passed between him and Ahmed he asked us for matches, and we gave him the box we had been furiously striking in our search for the palace frescoes.

112

Princess Muna on one of her London shopping expeditions

(above) Near the Qumran Caves, where the Dead Sea Scrolls were found in 1947

(above) Part of the Azraq Oasis. (left) A glimpse of the 'rose-red city', Petra, through the only approach to the ancient seat of kings

'Qasr Kharanah next,' said Ahmed and we swirled off again across the desert like a dust storm on wheels. We could see this castle from quite a distance, a mighty square-shaped building in pink stone, with rounded buttresses at each corner. It dominated the flat desert around it for miles. The arrow slits in the massively built walls gave it the appearance of a military fortress rather than a hunting lodge used for pleasure, but its grimness was relieved a little by a delicate frieze of bricks set in a herringbone pattern round the top of the walls.

The castle was locked, but Ahmed walked across to another black tent pitched nearby, and came back with the key. The man living there is paid by the Department of Antiquities to be gatekeeper and watchman, for although to us it seemed the castle was miles away from anywhere, it is on an ancient caravan route that is still used today by travellers from the north, especially the Haj buses coming down from Turkey and Northern Syria at the time of the annual pilgrimage to Mecca. These trans-desert travellers, like many others, had felt the urge to record their names and the date on plaster left clinging to the ancient walls inside until the Department put a lock on the door.

Once the castle door was opened, we found ourselves in a wide passage with narrow, vaulted rooms on either side. 'The stables,' Ahmed explained. Beyond was an open courtyard with flights of steps leading up to a maze of first floor rooms, some still in quite good order and decorated with arched alcoves and rosettes and zig-zag friezes carved in plaster. We wandered from room to room trying to imagine what each one had been used for. One looked like the interior of a small cathedral with pillars, niches and high vaulted ceiling, and might, we thought, have been the Caliph's reception room. More stairs led up to the roof where we had an eagle's eye view across miles of desert which we three and the gatekeeper and his family seemed to have entirely to ourselves.

Ahmed told us the gatekeeper had asked him when the next supply of water would arrive for the family's reserve was getting low. The water is sent across the desert by truck and is stored in a cistern. Although there must have been some natural source of water here at one time, otherwise the castle would not have been built, no trace of it has been found. Ahmed also told us that the castle was supposed to be haunted and people visiting it had seen ghostly dogs and horses in its crumbling courtyard. We saw nothing but a hawk wheeling high overhead in the sky that by now was almost white with the heat of the afternoon. We had time for only one more castle that day, Mushetta, and we had to hurry. Ahmed did not want to be caught out in the desert at night and neither did we.

Between Kharanah and Mushetta we passed an Army encampment and Ahmed said we were now getting close to the desert highway that leads from the Saudi border to Amman. We picked up a young soldier who was hitching a lift into the city and he seemed just as keen to look around this last castle as we were. Yes, he said, he knew about it, but had never had the chance to really look at it.

By the time we reached Mushetta the sun was beginning to set, turning the burnt bricks of which the castle is built into dark crimson. We climbed over a fallen pillar of green marble, and found beneath the walls and soaring arches that had supported the vanished roof many large blocks of golden stone beautifully carved with bunches of grapes entwined with vine leaves and flowers.

This desert palace had never been finished, although nothing has yet been found to show why. Perhaps the building had come to an abrupt end because of an earthquake, as it did on the summer palace of Caliph Hisham (Khirbet al Mafjar) in the Jordan Valley, three miles out of Jericho. Hisham's palace is the only one in Jordan that is not lost in the remoteness of the desert. He obviously preferred the suburban life, and a lush one too. None of the other castles had such superb mosaics and architecture as his. The famous and well-preserved Tree of Human Cruelty which shows three gazelles, one of them being attacked by a lion, grazing beneath a sinister looking tree that bears eyes instead of fruit, is one of the finest ancient mosaics in the world.

114

Mushetta is in a different style from Khirbet al Mafjar but both palaces would have been enormous and quite magnificent had they been completed.

Most of the carvings at Mushetta were stripped off and presented to Kaiser Wilhelm II by the Turkish Sultan, a souvenir to beat all souvenirs of the German ruler's visit to the Holy Land before the First World War. They were taken to a museum in Berlin and most of them were destroyed during the Second World War. Back in Amman the next morning the frescoes we had missed at Amra were described to us – hunting scenes showing saluki dogs, and a lion pulling down a wild ass, dancers, musicians, ladies of the harem, flowers, fruit and birds.

There was an odd little sequel, six months later, to this exhausting, frustrating and fascinating day among the desert castles. I was back in Jordan and admiring the hunting dogs, salukis, of an officer in the Jordan Army. 'One day I must go back to see the ones we missed on the walls of Amra,' I said. The officer asked me what time of the year we had been there and when I told him he said, 'So it was you. I received a report about then that a man and woman had been tearing around the desert, and wondered who they were.'

His remark underlined the fact that visitors to these lovely castles in the desert are so few that their progress is worth reporting. But the Jordan Government has plans to change this and put them on the tourist map. The oasis of Azraq and one thousand five hundred square miles of desert are now being turned into a national park to preserve the wild life and vegetation precariously hanging on, as well as the archaeological treasures.

Many of the animals and birds hunted by the Omayyad Caliphs have completely disappeared : ostriches, wild asses, bears, roedeer, antelope, oryx and the Asiatic lion which was a favourite subject in frescoes and mosaics. The Arabian gazelles, the smaller, Bambi-like Dorcas gazelles and the ibex have dwindled to a few herds and are in danger of being lost altogether. So are the desert jackals, foxes, and the turkey-sized Houbara bustards. Bedouin report the presence of cheetahs, although there can now

115

be literally only a handful left. The lion has not roamed this desert for about five hundred years.

Wholesale killing by automatic rifles fired from Land Rovers and fast cars is largely to blame for the final, rapid emptying of the desert. Even ten years ago large herds of gazelles were still seen. Heads would roll in anger if the old Caliphs were alive today to see how their sporting methods of hunting had degenerated.

Once the national park is well established and the wild life of the desert has had time to recover and multiply, experts see no reason why well-defined hunting areas around it should not then be established, as they have been beside the game reserves in Africa. But the hunting will be controlled and figuratively speaking heads will certainly roll if the huntsmen do not stick to the rules of sportsmanship.

The Samaritans

THERE IS A small community of about three hundred and fifty people, living in Nablus in the north of Jordan, which is gradually being squeezed out of existence because the strictness of its ancient religion prevents it from becoming part of the modern world, and the modern world, with many other things on its mind, is passing it by.

The people of this community are the Samaritans, the sect that provided the subject for perhaps the most famous of Christ's parables. They claim to be the only true descendants of the tribes of Israel and followers of the ancient Jewish faith, and they, like the desert gazelle, might have stepped straight out of the Old Testament.

Their ancestors, they say, were the few who were left behind when the city of Samaria, the capital of ancient Israel, was destroyed by the Assyrians in 720 BC and thousands of its inhabitants deported to Babylon and other cities in the Assyrian Empire. Their holy books are the Pentateuch – the first five books of the Old Testament, which embody the Law of Moses, although they recognise to some extent the Book of Joshua. Moses, they say, is the only Prophet of God and Mount Gerizim, which rises above Nablus, is their holy mountain and for them 'the navel of the earth'. They believe that on this mountain Joshua built the first Tabernacle, following God's commandment to Moses, and every Passover they still sacrifice lambs on its summit.

In the fifth century BC, refusing to recognise Solomon's Temple in Jerusalem as the true Temple, they broke away from the rest of the Jews and built a new Temple of their own on Gerizim, the Mountain of God. A bitter division between Jew and Samaritan grew so that by the time of Christ, Samaritan was an abusive word among the Jews, a far cry from the meaning it has had among Christians ever since Christ used it to illustrate what true charity means.

Paradoxically the stubborn courage that has helped the Samaritans to hang on to the strict code of their religion for nearly two thousand five hundred years looks as if it is going to become their death warrant, for they are finding it almost impossible to adapt their Biblical way of life to the twentieth century.

They are not allowed to marry outside their faith, which means that generations of inbreeding has weakened them, and their number is dwindling even more rapidly today because many of their young men and women are so poverty-stricken they are forced to stay single. Four years ago when the Religious Council of the Samaritan Sect in the Holy Land made an international appeal for funds to help them build their own school, they disclosed that thirty of their men and a similar number of women, all in their thirties and forties, were unable to marry 'because of lack of marriage prerequisites – food and lodging'.

Members of the sect can only eat food which has been prepared by one of themselves, so they are reluctant to leave their own community and seek work outside the Nablus area, away from their homes. The men are traditionally good craftsmen and those who have managed to find work are mostly in the tailoring or hand-made jewellery trades. But their priests, who are not allowed to do any kind of manual work, have to rely on charity to live. The High Priest is both their religious and civil head and under him is a council of priests and elders which acts as a parliament in conducting the affairs of the community.

The Jordan Government provides grants and does what it can to help the Samaritans, but has a far bigger struggle on its hands in helping the six hundred and fifty thousand Palestinian refugees that are in the country. So on the whole the Samaritans are left to their own resources and to charity, but centuries of being virtually imprisoned inside their own faith has brought them to the point where it is difficult for them to help themselves.

'It is time the Christians applied the parable of the Good Samaritan to the Samaritans,' a Biblical scholar who lives in London, and who has made a study of their history, said to me at the time when he was helping them to raise money for their school and finding it hard going. 'It is an urgent matter now of saving an ancient sect, the people whom Christ loved, from extinction.'

The school, which has been built at last, is something the Samaritans feel is essential for them to have. Although the Jordan Government schools are open to Samaritan children, the sect wanted its own teachers to teach them in its own language, an ancient dialect of West Aramaic, and according to its own laws. Until their school was open many of the children did not get any formal schooling because of this. Now the Samaritans hope they can educate their children to the point where they can get good jobs and begin to help the rest of the community to stand on its own feet. But this is going to take time, and more years yet of living on the bread line.

In the meantime, some of the Samaritans eke out a living by forecasting the future. They have a reputation for being expert fortune-tellers and some of the local women go to them for 'advice'. Some foreigners go too. The day I visited them, one offered to read my future 'by numbers'. All he needed from me was my full name, my birthdate and six weeks to work out the forecast and he promised to send me the result. But I refused. The future is something I prefer to take as it comes.

In spite of my refusal, the Samaritans were kind and gentle hosts and patiently answered my questions about their history. They showed me the ancient silver decorated scrolls of their version of the Pentateuch which they believe are the oldest hand-written books in the world, far older than the more famous Dead Sea scrolls. But sadly their claim is not accepted by scholars who have seen them and who date their scrolls as tenth century AD although they have been copied from a far older source. But they are old, very beautiful and precious. At one time the Samaritans

119

owned manuscripts dating back to before the fourth century AD but most of them are now in the British Museum and the Vatican Library.

They are a spectacularly tall and handsome people and their elders look even taller, in their full length Biblical robes, flowing beards and high red turbans. They eagerly discussed the great hopes they had in their school and what it could do for them. As they talked, one could see how these gentle giants were finding it hard to adapt their way of life to the twentieth century without modernising their religion and giving up their most cherished principles. Much of the rest of the world has managed to do it, but I suppose we have compromised in the progress, and this is something they will not do.

During the Roman occupation of Palestine Samaritans could be found in scattered communities all over the Roman Empire, but they suffered so many oppressions that by the sixteenth century AD they were already a dwindling people and they began to abandon their outlying settlements and gather at Nablus, near their ancient sanctuary. During this century a few families moved to Tel Aviv and Jaffa, but the majority of the Samaritans are still in Nablus.

Nablus is built on the site of Flavia Neapolis, one of the cities of Roman Palestine, at the foot of Mount Gerizim, and is the modern commercial centre for the old district of Samaria. Orchards, olive groves and vineyards surround it, and the whole area is so steeped in the history of the Patriarchs and the Prophets that the present day Samaritans, with their Old Testament way of life, hardly come as a surprise.

Just outside Nablus, on the road in from Jerusalem, is the village of Balatah, the site of the Biblical Shechem, which was a Canaanite town when Abraham arrived there with his family, pitched his tents and build the first altar to God. His grandson Jacob camped outside Shechem and dug a well there and Jacob's son, Joseph, was buried nearby after the Israelites had brought his mummy with them from Egypt, at the time of the Exodus, nearly four hundred years later.

120

It was Jacob's well from which the Samaritan woman drew water for Christ. The well is now enclosed by a Greek Orthodox Church and the monk in charge will let down a pail and draw up water for visitors. The water is cold, clear and refreshing, even though Jacob dug the well nearly four thousand years ago.

The site of the city of Samaria, built in the ninth century BC as his capital, by Omri, King of the Biblical Northern Kingdom of Israel, is on a hill about six miles north of Nablus near the village of Sabastya. Omri bought the hill, from which you can see right across the coastal plain of Palestine to the Mediterranean, from a man called Shemer, for two talents of silver. His son, Ahab, enlarged and improved the city, built a house of ivory for his Phoenician wife, Jezebel, and fell foul of the Prophet Elijah because among other things, he put up a temple to Baal to please his Queen.

Elijah's prophecies that Ahab's blood would be licked by the dogs and Jezebel would be eaten by them came true. Ahab was killed by an arrow in a battle against Syria and when his men washed his blood stained armour and chariot in the pool of Samaria, the city's dogs gathered around to lick up the blood. Jezebel was thrown from one of the windows of her castle by eunuchs during the rebellion of Jehu against Ahab's successor, and Jehu's horse trampled her underfoot. When they looked for her remains afterwards to bury her, remembering that in spite of everything she had been a King's daughter, all they could find were her skull, her feet and the palms of her hands. The dogs had taken the rest.

Sargon II, the Assyrian king, captured Samaria more than a hundred years later, and after a three-year siege, carried the inhabitants off into captivity in 720 BC. It was after the Israelites started filtering back into Palestine some generations later that the split occurred between the Jews and the Samaritans. The returning Jews claimed that the Samaritans were the descendants of the people the Assyrians had settled in the land in their own place.

Samaria was rebuilt, only to be destroyed again by Alexander the Great and then it was the turn of the Romans to rebuild it, in

121

the first century BC. Caesar Augustus gave it to Herod the Great who renamed it Sebaste and made it his capital. The imposing pillars and ruined walls built of great blocks of stone that still stand on the outskirts of Sabastya are all that are left of Herod's once splendid Roman city.

Excavations near the Roman ruins have uncovered the foundation of the city that Omri built. But perhaps the most fascinating discoveries have been many pieces of ivory that once decorated the palace Ahab built for Jezebel. These ivory pieces are carved with scenes that are very like those you can see painted on the walls of the pyramids and temples of Egypt – kneeling girls with bare breasts and finely pleated hipster skirts, palm trees, flowers and animals. Some of the ivory pieces were high-lighted with gold leaf and inset with glass and paste 'jewels'. You can see them in the Palestine Archaeological Museum in Jerusalem.

Ahab's ivory palace must have been the envy of his neighbouring kings, but it still was not enough for him. The Bible tells how he went into a sulk refusing to eat and turning his face to the wall, because Naboth the Jezreelite would not let him have a vineyard that was alongside another palace he had built in the northern Samarian town of Jezreel. Ahab wanted it for a herb garden to enlarge his palace grounds, but Naboth stubbornly refused to part with the vineyard that had belonged to his ancestors. So Jezebel tricked the people into stoning Naboth to death and again roused the fury of her old enemy, Elijah, who confronted Ahab as he was inspecting his newly acquired vineyard and prophesied the sticky ends for him and his Queen.

Elijah's apprentice, the Prophet Elisha, is remembered in another place, not far from Nablus – Beitin. This little village has been identified as the Biblical town of Bethel, the place where Elisha was mocked by the children because he was bald. 'Go up, bald head', they yelled after him, as he walked up the street, and he turned round and cursed them. Immediately two she-bears came out of the forest and tore forty-two of the village children to pieces. Terrible retribution for a childish prank, but the children have their own memorial in the Convent of the Youths, which is near the village.

It was in Bethel too that Jacob lay down to sleep on a pillar of stone and in a dream saw a ladder reaching from earth to heaven. The stone on which he slept is said to be the Coronation Stone of Scone that is under the Coronation Throne of the Kings and Queens of England, in Westminster Abbey. Tradition has it that the Stone was taken to Tara in Ireland, and then to Scone in Scotland. Edward I carried it off from Scotland and brought it to Westminster and apart from the time when it was stolen by a group of Scottish Nationalists and taken back to Scotland, three years before the coronation of Queen Elizabeth II, it has been there ever since.

Jerash, Roman City in the Desert

A SMALL COPPER coin with the helmeted head of a Roman soldier on one side and a long legged she-wolf suckling the twins Romulus and Remus on the other, is one of my treasures from Jordan. I got it in exchange for a handful of modern coins from a small boy who tagged on as I was exploring the spectacularly lovely ruins of Jerash that lie in a valley among the mountains of Gilead, about thirty miles north-east of Amman.

Jerash was called Gerⅽsa in Christ's time and was a provincial Roman city, built over an earlier Hellenistic one, on the very outskirts of the Empire. It was magnificently laid out with wide streets, elegant colonnades, temples and theatres, a forum, stadium and public baths, and rich from the trade brought to it by the caravans coming up from Petra on their way to Damascus. Like Petra, it was lost to the western world after the Crusades and rediscovered at the beginning of the nineteenth century. As it was uncovered it was found to be the most perfectly preserved example of a Roman provincial city in the whole of the Middle East.

Unlike many other ancient cities it was not thoroughly pulled to pieces by later inhabitants in search of stone which they could use to build houses and village walls, and although it has been damaged by earthquakes, an astonishing amount of it still stands. Magnificent columns, arches and temples are silhouetted against the sky as you approach on the road from Amman. The great triple gateway of the triumphal arch which was built to celebrate Hadrian's visit to the city in 129 AD is right alongside the road

124

and although the highest points have tumbled down, you can still walk through the central arch under which the Emperor rode with pomp and ceremony.

The Greek goddess Artemis was worshipped in Jerash and her temple with its impressive stairway and soaring columns rises high above the city. But the most spectacular ruin is that of the vast horseshoe-shaped forum, the ancient market place where the citizens gathered to bargain for the camel loads of spices, gold, ivory, precious stones and ostrich feathers brought up by the caravans from Egypt and Southern Arabia. Its paving is still intact and much of its surrounding colonnade still stands.

The wide Street of Columns which divides the city from north to south, leads out from the forum and is also still paved with its original stones. In places you can see the grooves left by the heavy, iron-shod wheels of the chariots that used to clatter up and down the street, scattering citizens, camels, donkeys and dogs who jay-walked in their path.

Recently many of the street's columns which were shaken down by earthquakes more than a thousand years ago have been put back by the Royal Engineers of Jordan's Army, under the direction of the Department of Antiquities. Since each column is made up of a base and three segments, each weighing between seven and ten tons, the crews had a few fraught moments as the great carved cylinders were swung into place by heavy cranes. The Roman engineers who first put them up would have marvelled to see today's soldiers putting them back at the rate of five a day, but the soldiers in their turn have been equally impressed at what the Romans were able to achieve without the help of modern machinery.

The soldiers and archaeologists have uncovered other streets in the city too, and in one of them, a shop containing remains of a furnace and fragments of elegant pottery. They are still at work clearing and reconstructing the old network of Roman aqueducts, canals and pools which were fed by the many springs in the hills around, and the Golden River, the grandly named small stream that flows through Jerash.

125

The Romans used this plentiful supply of water for ornamental fountains, luxurious steam baths and a deep pool the size of a small lake on which they boated and held water sports. As Rome declined, Byzantine churches were built over the pagan temples and every year the Christians of Jerash celebrated the anniversary of the miracle of Cana, when water in the city's ancient fountains was said to turn into wine. But even in the sixth century, when many of the citizens of Jerash were staunch Christians, the lavish water supply of the city still roused dark instincts in some, and pagan water festivals that included the voluptuous freedom of mixed bathing were still being celebrated and shocking the pious.

After the armies of Islam arrived in Jerash a century later, the statues, paintings and many of the fine mosaic pictures of the Byzantine churches were destroyed by a movement that thought it sacriligious to reproduce the human form, and earthquakes in the eighth century AD continued the devastation of Roman and Byzantine buildings alike. The city was eventually deserted but flashed briefly into history again during the Crusades when the Arabs converted the Temple of Artemis into a fortress which was captured and destroyed by the Crusader King of Jerusalem, Baldwin II.

Strangely enough the plentiful water supply and the fertile land of the valley around Jerash did not tempt later generations to resettle the site. It was left ruined and empty for nearly a thousand years and was gradually covered by the sand ladened winds that blow in from the desert a few miles away to the east.

Then at the end of the nineteenth century, after the Russian war against the Caucasus, a group of Circassian Moslem refugees settled there. Fortunately they decided to build their village on the east bank of the Golden River, the side on which the citizens of ancient Jerash had lived too. All the beautiful and important public buildings had been built on the west bank and most of them were still there, under a thousand years accumulation of soil and sand.

The first serious excavations of Jerash began in the 1920s but the archaeologists found very little trace of the Hellenistic city that preceded the Roman one and which was one of the Decapolis, the league of ten free cities in the Seleucid Kingdom of Syria. Philadephia, now Amman, was also one of them and so were Arbila (now Irbid) and Gadara the city overlooking the Sea of Galilee where Christ freed the man possessed of a legion of devils which then entered a herd of swine and caused them to run violently down a steep place into the sea. The ruins of Roman Gadara are now called Umm Quais and are in the north-east corner of Jordan on a hill that sheers down to the Sea of Galilee, and which is still the haunt of wild pig.

But although Arbila and Gadara were greater in their heyday than Jerash, these ancient cities have almost disappeared. And in Amman, apart from the Roman amphitheatre and a few remains of Hellenistic and Roman buildings on the Citadel, little is left to show what Philadephia looked like in its golden age too. Only Jerash still stands, its tall stone columns silhouetted against the blue sky and the hills of Gilead, wild marigolds and anemones growing at its feet, an almost perfectly preserved Roman city on the edge of the Arabian desert.

'It will rival Pompeii by the time we have finished excavating and reconstructing,' one of the archaeological assistants at the Amman Museum told me when I went in with my Roman coin to ask if they could identify it and whether or not they needed to record it. Antiquities acquired like this, or found, should be reported in case they are an important missing link in reconstructing the past.

The museum not only dated the coin as fifth century AD, they also cleaned it up and gave me two others to go with it. Since much that is old is contantly being found in Jordan, the museums in Amman and Jerusalem occasionally sell to the public a few small, surplus things like coins and clay lamps, when they have all the specimens of that particular item that they need. It is one way of keeping their display cabinets and storage rooms from overflowing and for tourists it is a sure way of acquiring accurately dated and genuine antiques at a fair price.

127

Amman

PERHAPS NOWHERE IN the Roman Empire did the Legions feel more at home than in Philadephia, the name by which they knew Amman. Like Rome, it is built on seven hills. Like Rome it was embellished with fine paved streets, colonnaded plazas, baths, temples and theatres. Even the climate is similar enough to Rome to have made the Legions happy in the thought that they might have been posted to far worse places, Londinium for instance, with its damp summers and cold, foggy winters.

The Romans were in Philadephia for four hundred years but apart from the spectacular and well-preserved open air theatre which the Emperor Trajan had built at the foot of one of the seven hills and which can still seat six thousand people for modern presentations of entertainment, little is left of the city's Roman glory. An odeum, a smaller, covered theatre, has been found in the gardens of the Philadephia Hotel across the road from the open air theatre. There are ruins of the Temple of Hercules on Citadel Hill and of a nymphaeum over the stream that runs through the down-town vegetable market.

But this rapidly spreading capital that is growing at such a rate that even the locals joke they cannot find their way around after a weekend out of town, has long since spilled over the area covered by the Roman city and the even smaller site, on Citadel Hill, which was the Biblical Rabbath Ammon, capital of the Ammonites. A museum stands on top of Citadel Hill now, and somewhere near it the Ammonites after they had defeated Og, King of Bashan, must have triumphantly displayed their strange battle trophy, Og's great iron bedstead. Og, says the Bible, was the only one that remained of the giants and his bed was nine cubits long and four cubits wide. A cubit was the length of a man's arm from wrist to elbow, anything between eighteen and twenty-two inches, so Og must have been quite large.

Some two hundred years later Uriah the Hittite, Bathsheba's husband, died outside the Citadel walls, leaving it conveniently clear for David to marry his beautiful widow. David had sent messengers to the King of Rabbath Ammon to comfort him on the death of his father, but the King was suspicious and insulted the messengers in a most undignified way. Their beards were half-shaved off and their clothes cut short, 'even to their buttocks', and like this they were sent back to David, who declared war at once. Seizing the chance to kill two birds with one stone, David ordered that Uriah should be 'set in the forefront of the hottest battle . . . that he may be smitten and die'. The eventual outcome of this murderous treachery was King Solomon, the son that Bathsheba had after she became David's wife.

All traces of the Old Testament city were destroyed by the Romans when they started building on Citadel Hill, but the museum, which has been cleverly incorporated into the still standing ruins of Roman, Byzantine and early Arabic buildings, has on display some sherds dating from this period that were dug up on the slopes of the hill.

Until 1921 when the Emir Abdullah decided to make Amman the capital of Transjordan, it was just a small town known chiefly as a Circassian settlement and an important camel market. Bedouin sheiks and tribesmen used to wander through the souks spending the money they had got for their camels on trinkets and stores to take back to the desert. Now there are many fine shops selling goods from all over the world, air-conditioned hotels with nightclubs and swimming pools, a new university, opulent embassies, modern villas surrounded by beautiful gardens, boxing matches and drama festivals in the Roman theatre, an international airport, and traffic jams. It is a modern and completely Arab city, quite different in character from the international and tourist orientated city of Jerusalem. If you want to get the real feel of contemporary life in Jordan and have not much time to spend, Amman is the place to visit if only for a day.

Since it does not get the same crowds of tourists that Jerusalem and Bethlehem do, this is the place to shop, but don't try bargaining over the prices. This is a custom long since dead in the sophisticated capital of Jordan. The fascination of contrast is there though. Tiny goldsmith's shops filled with bangles, necklaces and earrings are just as likely to have in stock the latest models in Swiss watches as those old-fashioned 'harem' rings which are five jewel-studded bands of gold joined together at the back so that they are not entirely separated. The camera shops have the newest models too and all the photographic equipment anyone needs. On the shelves in the drapery shops you can find brocaded silks from Damascus alongside contemporary cottons from Switzerland and France.

There are Bedouin tribesmen and smartly suited businessmen in the streets, veiled women window shopping and pretty girls in bikinis around the pools at the Al Urdon and Philadephia hotels. You can eat *hummus, kebabs* and 'ladies' fingers', or if you are feeling less adventurous, smoked salmon, steak and ice-cream. And before you get your early morning tea and newspaper in the hotel you are likely to have been woken long before by the muezzin's dawn-call to prayer from the city's minarets that seem strategically placed so that the noise bounces off the hills as if they were sounding boards.

Amman is a good centre for touring holidays too. Jerash, Jericho, the Dead Sea, Jerusalem, Bethlehem, Karak and Madaba can be seen in half a day's trip out of the city. Petra can be done in one hectic day, returning in time for dinner when the lights of the city, sprinkled over the hillsides, will be a sight almost as breathtaking as the rose-red necropolis.

The population of Amman has tripled since 1948 and is now about three hundred and thirty thousand. The city is already spreading outwards to the fringe of the desert which starts a few miles away to the east. Except when the khamsin blows, it is hard to believe that the desert is on the doorstep, surrounded as you are in the city with all the trappings of modern life. The kham-sin is the hot, gritty wind that blows straight in from the desert usually at the beginning of summer, bringing with it a reminder that half an hour's drive away from the air-conditioned hotels and offices and the busy streets the twentieth century comes to a stop.

Roman paving and drains, commonplace finds as bulldozers and drills clear areas in the city to make way for modern buildings, are other reminders of another way of life, but hardly rate a second glance, except from the Department of Antiquities. But a few months ago most people's imagination was caught by a strange archaeological discovery five miles out of the city, and one that has caused Turkey to start re-examining its claim to have the site of the cave of the legendary Seven Sleepers.

The Sleepers were seven Christian youths who about 250 AD, during a period of Christian persecution in the Middle East, hid in a cave. Their hiding place was discovered and the entrance to the cave blocked, and the young men were left to die and be glori-fied as martyrs. Over two hundred years later a herdsman re-opened the cave and as the sunlight poured in the seven youths, who like Rip Van Winkle had slept for two centuries and not died after all, awoke. One of them went into town to look for food and was astonished to find the Cross over the city gates and to hear Christ's name openly spoken in the streets with the people show-ing no fear of persecution. They in their turn were astonished at this strange youth in old-fashioned clothes who tried to shop with coins that were two hundred years old.

As the Sleepers' story became known, the local Christian com-munity declared that God had caused this miracle to happen to confirm their faith in the resurrection of the dead. The Seven Sleepers lived their normal span, none the worse for time having stood still for them for two hundred years, and when they even-tually died the Byzantine Emperor Theodosius II is said to have had them buried in the cave that was their bedchamber for so long, and a church built over it.

This legend was widespread in ancient Syria in the early part of the Christian era. But although Amman is in what was then Syria, tradition for many centuries has held that the site of the Seven Sleepers' cave is near the ancient city of Ephesus in Anatolia.

The cave outside Amman that Jordan's Department of Antiquities is now excavating shows signs of a fifth-century Byzantine building directly over it, which later might have been used as a mosque and originally been a church. Other finds on the site have been graves with Byzantine and Roman inscriptions on their stones, copper pieces of Roman and early Islamic money and a stone tablet, probably of the ninth century AD, inscribed with something in early Arabic that so far has not been deciphered. The Department has asked the Turkish Government for photographs and a full description of their cave at Ephesus, so that a comparison can be made and checked against ancient records of the legends.

Many legends are based on happenings that could not be properly understood at the time and this one might have been the result of finding the bodies of the seven young martyrs perfectly preserved by the atmospheric conditions of the cave for two hundred years after their death. Whatever the origin of the story might be, the antiquities departments of Jordan and Turkey are now trying to discover which country has the better claim to the spot on which the martyrdom happened.

As Amman grew into a twentieth-century capital, Citadel Hill, the hub of the city since Biblical days, was gradually left to its memory and its museum, and Jebel Amman, another of the seven hills, began to take its place. Most of the new Government offices have been built on its slopes and this is the most fashionable district in which to live. It is on Jebel Amman where the Prime Minister has his office and where the Government meets. There are two legislative chambers, the House of Representatives whose members are voted in by the electorate, male citizens of Jordan over the age of eighteen, and the Senate whose members are appointed by the King.

The problems the Government has had to face since 1950 when

the Royal Hashemite Kingdom of Jordan came into being have been enormous. Practically overnight the population of the country was doubled when refugees from Palestine poured in, three-quarters of them farmers and unskilled workers, with little hope of livelihood in a country that is short of rain and natural resources and had lost its traditional trade routes to the Mediterranean after the armistice line was drawn up.

Pulling herself up by her boot strings, Jordan has made great economic strides since then. Other Arab countries around her have grown rich through the discovery of oil, but so far none has been found in Jordan. Agriculture is the backbone of the economy, as it has always been throughout the country's history, the livelihood on which most of its population depends. In spite of years of drought, only sixteen inches of rainfall on average and less than five meagre inches over the desert which spreads across the greater part of the country, crops of wheat, barley, vegetables, fruit, tobacco, and olive oil have consistently increased.

Agricultural experimental stations under the direction of the Ministry of Agriculture are bringing the farmers up to date on modern and efficient methods of cultivation, irrigation, cropping and pest control. Parts of the desert are beginning to bloom in defiance of harsh, natural conditions. But all the time more water is needed to improve the land already being farmed and to open up new agricultural areas, particularly in the Jordan Valley, if the farmers are going to go on increasing their standard of living and the country is to prosper.

Apart from Jordan's irrigation schemes for using the River Jordan, the Government Water Authority is developing all possible water resources in the country, even in the seemingly bone-dry southern part of the desert where there are signs of underground supplies. New wells are being drilled to tap this lifeblood and ancient wells and water systems, some dating back to Roman times, are being repaired and made to work again.

The Government is striving to increase industrial projects and to make the most of the country's natural resources. Valuable minerals are soon to be extracted from the Dead Sea, phosphate is being mined, marble quarried and deposits of manganese, iron, gypsum, and copper are being explored by geologists.

Tourism is an important factor in the country's economy as well, and one which has enormous potential. The climate is right, the fascination of Biblical and historical places is unbeaten by any other country, the scenery is a photographer's paradise and travel facilities are constantly and rapidly increasing.

All these things are planned and directed from Amman, the hub of a new and developing country, and yet a city that has played its part in the progress of civilisation for nearly ten thousand years.

Crusader Trail

'WE WERE THROWN out of Palestine in 1291 and in 1880 decided it was time we re-established our ties with the Holy Land. Two years later, in 1882, we founded a hospital in Jerusalem.' A member of the Order of St John of Jerusalem in the British Realm, the modern descendents of those Crusader knights who called themselves the Hospitallers, was telling me how their famous eye hospital in Jerusalem, one of the finest of its kind in the world, came into being.

The Hospitallers – the Knights of St John – were military monks who divided their time in the twelfth and thirteenth centuries between fighting to free the Christian shrines in the Holy Land, protecting pilgrims with the sword, and peacefully running a hospital in Jerusalem which they built close to the Church of the Holy Sepulchre in an area now known as the Muristan, and later another in Acre, on the Palestine coast.

Inside their Convent, as the members of the Order called their compound of church, monastery and hospital, these knights wore black robes embroidered on the left breast with an eight-pointed cross. On the battlefield they wore over their armour a red surcoat decorated with a plain white cross and carried a banner bearing a white cross on a red background. Unlike many of the fuedal Crusader knights who were more interested in claiming land for themselves in Palestine than fighting for Christianity, these battling monks were dedicated to their holy war. Celibate, scorning the gorgeous trappings and gay life that soon became fashionable among many of the Crusaders, and according to a chronicler of

135

the period, 'washing but seldom', they won the respect even of their enemies.

A traveller to Jerusalem in 1160 wrote: 'Over against the Church of the Holy Sepulchre on the opposite side of the way towards the south is a hospital where in various rooms is collected together a great multitude of sick people, both men and women, who are tended and restored to health daily at very great expense. When I was there I learned that the whole number of these sick people amount to two thousand.' This hospital belonged to the Order of St John and served the poor as well as the sick. Thirty poor people were fed there every day and every year one thousand warm lambskin cloaks were handed out to the needy.

When the gallant Moslem leader Saladin captured Jerusalem from the Crusaders in 1187, he admired the fighting spirit of the Hospitallers so much that he allowed them a twelve months' breathing space to settle the affairs of their hospital before expelling them from the city. They retreated to the castle of Margat in Syria, where they set up a new Convent, and later were forced back to Acre where they built another hospital larger than their old one in Jerusalem. From here and the Krak of the Knights, the massive Crusader castle still standing in Lebanon, they held out for nearly another hundred years, until 1291 and the last great siege of the Crusades.

Now, eight hundred years later they are back in the Holy Land, though not as knights or monks, but as founders and supporters of a great charitable organisation that runs a hospital and research unit dedicated to fighting blindness and eye disease in the Middle East. Already the research unit team has isolated and identified the virus that causes the dreaded trachoma, a disease of the eye which is the greatest cause of blindness in many parts of the world and which in some areas of the Middle East affects over ninety per cent of all children before they are five years old. Effective drugs for its treatment are being used and the team is now working on the production of a vaccine to immunise people against the disease.

If it does become possible to wipe out trachoma, as diphtheria, cholera, typhoid and malaria have been virtually eliminated in other parts of the world, the benefit to mankind would be tremendous, not only in the Middle East but also in parts of Africa, Asia, India, Australia and South America where this eye affliction is prevalent. When the World Health Organisation took a recent census in the small country of Tunisia it was found that trachoma was the cause of forty million man hours being lost every year, so the social benefit alone to a country freed from this scourge would be tremendous.

The Order of St John of Jerusalem in the British Realm which still uses the eight-pointed, white cross of the Crusader Hospitallers as its emblem, built the present eye hospital and research centre in 1960 in a new suburb of Jerusalem, on the way to the airport. The old hospital which was established outside the Jaffa Gate on the Order's return to the Holy Land at the end of the last century had to be abandoned during the Arab-Jewish war and is now on the other side of the armistice line. The foundation of the Hospitallers' twelfth-century Convent is gradually being brought to light by excavations in the Muristan area near the Church of the Holy Sepulchre, to add to the other impressive remains of Crusader times in Jordan.

In Jerusalem the Crusaders' greatest monument is the present outline of the Church of the Holy Sepulchre. They brought the motley collection of churches, chapels and grottoes together under one great roof and added a belfry. Their stronghold in the city was a fortress built on the site of the ancient Citadel which is beside the Jaffa Gate. The north-eastern tower of the Citadel is called the Tower of David, although it dates from the time of Herod the Great, and the Crusaders built on to it, giving the Citadel its present plan. But their fortress was largely destroyed by the Moslems in the thirteenth century and now only some of the foundation stones are left.

They turned the Mosque of the Dome of the Rock into a Christian church, which became the church of the Templars, an Order of Knights originally founded to protect pilgrims on their hazardous journey from the Palestine coast to Jerusalem. The Temple

137

museum's beautiful iron grill, until recently around the sacred rock, is Crusader work. The Knights Templar and the Crusader Kings of Jerusalem also used the underground vaults in the Haram area surrounding the Mosque as store rooms and stables for their horses.

But the quaintest reminder of the Crusaders in Jerusalem is the name of the Souk el Attarin in the heart of the Old City. In Crusader days part of this Souk was called Herbs Street, and the description is retained in the Arabic name. The street that they wryly called Malcuisinat – Bad Cookery – is still occupied by pastry and sweetmeat shops, but with a far better reputation than they had eight hundred years ago.

Once they had captured Jerusalem the Crusaders built a chain of fortresses on the eastern side of the River Jordan, the territory they called La Terre Oultre-Jordain, in the mountains of Moab and along the line of the Wadi Arabah, the great cleft that divides the Negeb and the eastern deserts and opens out like the mouth of a river on to the shores of the Red Sea at Aqaba. From these strongholds at Karak, Tafila, Shaubek, Petra, Aqaba and even in the Red Sea on a tiny, rocky island that they called the Isle de Graye, the Crusaders were able to patrol the route to Jerusalem from the south and at the same time make a handsome profit, just as the citizens of Petra had done a thousand years before, in claiming tribute from the caravans travelling up the ancient spice road from Southern Arabia.

Before the new Desert Highway was built, the old road to Petra followed the line of these southern castles of the Crusaders, which still rise massively above the flat-roofed Arab towns and villages that have grown around them. In spring it is more than likely that parts of the road south of Karak have been cracked open into miniature ravines or washed away altogether by the flash floods of winter. But one day at the beginning of April I took a chance on this and set out on a Crusader trail with some friends who were going to Petra. We bought a picnic of olives, cheese, meat and still-warm Arab bread from a delicatessen in Amman and headed first for Karak, the Crusaders' great Pierre du Désert.

The old walled town is built on the crest of a hill and the battlements of the ruined castle rise straight out of the bare, hilltop rocks. In front of the castle gates is a filled-in moat. Inside, the castle is a twilight world of stone-vaulted chambers, halls, corridors and stables. Here in times of peace the knights and their ladies lived in oriental splendour, dressing in fine silks and fur-lined cloaks, drinking the wines of Palestine out of jewelled goblets and riding over the fertile farmlands and bare high mountains around Karak with their hunting hawks and dogs as the old Caliphs had done in the eastern desert many generations before them.

In times of siege, the great castle could shelter the neighbouring Syrians who farmed the district under the castle lords, as well as all their flocks, and an enormous garrison. Sometimes, in spite of the battles raging outside the walls, the feasting and merry-making went on as before inside the vaulted rooms. Reynald de Chatillon, one of the Crusader lords of Karak, held a wedding party inside the castle in 1183 for his stepson, seventeen-year-old Humphrey of Toron, while Saladin was attacking the fortress.

The singing and dancing of the marriage celebrations were punctuated by the constant crack of Saladin's men bombarding the castle walls with rocks flung from their mangonels, but the bridegroom's mother, Lady Stephanie, calmly went on helping to prepare the bridal feast and sent out to Saladin dishes she had cooked herself. In gallant return he asked in which tower the bridal pair would be sleeping that night, and then ordered his men not to bombard it. On this occasion the castle was relieved by the army of Baldwin II, King of Jerusalem, which had marched down from the city through the Moabite hills. But five years later the castle eventually fell to the Moslems after a siege lasting almost a year. The defenders were starving to death by the time the gates were finally opened to the enemy.

From the crumbling outer walls of the castle we had a magnificent view, three thousand feet high, across the valley that runs up from Karak to the Dead Sea. The gate-keeper told us that in the days of the Crusaders, prisoners used to be thrown from the walls into the valley below. So that they would not die too quickly, wooden boxes were fastened over their heads as a mocking protection.

Outside the castle gates our car had attracted a bunch of small boys who were playing with the most ingenious home-made toy I have ever seen, a contraption of strong wire on wheels made from empty shoe-blacking tins that they trundled over the stony street with quite a clatter. Pulling this fascinating toy behind them, they ran after our car waving and shouting until something else attracted them, and they suddenly wheeled off down a side street.

We found the perfect spot for our picnic lunch, on the side of the mountain road just outside Karak, where the rocky ground was covered with purple-black irises, the loveliest of Jordan's wild spring flowers, and low growing hollyhocks. Biting into a meat sandwich, our driver suddenly withdrew his teeth and demanded to know whether or not he was 'eating pig'. I had forgotten that pork was forbidden to Moslems when shopping that morning, and had no idea what was inside the highly seasoned picnic sausage that I had bought. So he played safe and stuck to the cheese and olives. But the thought that it might have been a pork sandwich that he had put into his mouth worried him. After we had set off again he stopped in front of the mosque in the little village of Mazar and disappeared inside.

The mosque, with its bright green dome and twin minarets, looked opulently out of character with the rest of the village and our driver explained why when he came back. It was, he said, the burial place of three important followers of the Prophet who were killed nearby in a battle during Islam's holy war against the Byzantines. The present mosque was built about ten years ago when a much older mosque over the tombs was pulled down.

Until now the road surface had been good in spite of heavy rain some weeks before, but from Mazar, as it began to drop down towards the bed of the Wadi Hasa, it showed signs of recent flooding which would not have troubled a Land Rover, but which slowed our car down to a crawl in places.

The limestone mountains of Moab gave way to golden-brown sandstone crags and the valley bed was clouded with the pink blossoms of oleanders. The town of Tafila, almost hidden by olive groves, was on the other side of the valley and above the flat topped houses we could see the ruins of the Crusader keep. But with only two hours of daylight left and the cracks in the road getting wider, we decided to drive on to Shaubek in the Idumaean hills where Baldwin I, the first Crusader King of Jerusalem, built the castle of Montreal and from where he marched south to Petra and then to the Red Sea. Baldwin built small garrisons on the red rocks of Petra, and off the sea shore at Aqaba on the Isle de Graye which guarded the narrow Gulf of Aqaba. But Montreal was his great stronghold from which he was able to control the ancient caravan highway from Southern Arabia and Egypt to Damascus.

Like Karak, Montreal eventually was besieged to the point of starvation and capitulation, but not before the garrison had turned blind and helpless through lack of salt. The same Lady Stephanie, who a few years earlier had sent wedding feast dishes out to Saladin as he was besieging Karak, was, as heiress of Oultre-Jordain, the Chatelaine of Montreal as well as Karak. Her son, Humphrey of Toron, had been captured by Saladin who promised to release him if Lady Stephanie would order her garrisons at Karak and Montreal to surrender. She agreed and Humphrey was set free, but she could not make the garrisons obey her order to give in, so she sent her son back to Saladin saying she had failed in her side of the bargain. Chivalry was repaid by chivalry once again, and after the capitulation of both castles, Saladin released Humphrey once more and sent him back to his mother.

By the time we were within a few miles of Shaubek and its Crusader castle we realised that like Lady Stephanie we too were fighting a losing battle. The state of the road had forced us to make so many detours that we knew it would be dark before we reached the town. When we arrived all we could see was the massive loom of Montreal on the crest of a hill, making a dramatic silhouette against the dark blue evening sky. But perhaps this was the best way to see it, for the archaeologist, G Lankester Harding, in his book, *Antiquities of Jordan,* dismisses it as being impressive from a distance but hardly repaying a closer view.

From Shaubek to Wadi Musa and Petra we were driving along the tops of the mountains of ancient Edom, the highest mountain range in Jordan, which rises to five thousand three hundred feet above sea level, but the air was so clear we could easily see the lights of the supper fires in the valleys below. Snow falls heavily on these mountains some winters, blocking the passes and sometimes cutting off the villagers and Bedouin for weeks on end. When this happens there are serious losses of sheep and goats. Food and warm clothing have to be dropped to the snow besieged families by the Jordan Air Force and invariably King Hussein leads the relief operations, piloting his own helicopter and pinpointing the places where the bundles should land.

Until 1914 these mountains had been covered with forests but during the First World War the trees were cut down by the Turks and used to fuel their troop and supply trains on the Hejaz railway. In the last few years Jordan's Forestry Department has started an ambitious plan of re-afforestation which will be helped by the recent announcement that eight hundred square miles of the mountains and valleys from Petra to Shaubek are to be made a National Park where the vegetation and wild life will be protected. Leopards used to prowl the sun-baked rocks of Petra and the mountains of Edom. Perhaps the odd one still does, as the local villagers and Bedouin firmly believe. But wolves, foxes and hyenas are certainly there and now maybe the leopards the Crusader knights knew and some adopted into their coats of arms will gradually come back to their old hunting ground.

Frontier Villages

THE AVERAGE TOURIST in Jordan is hardly aware of the bitterness of the hostility that exists between the Jordanians and the Israelis. Even in Jerusalem where barbed wire and the scar of no man's land divides the city, the atmosphere is phlegmatic. Jerusalem seems inured by history to trouble and sorrow. At the city's Mandelbaum Gate, the only place on the entire three hundred and fifty-mile-long truce line where tourists and pilgrims can pass from one country into the other, but only one way, for there is no returning, the bitter division comes home forcibly. But even then it is somehow modulated by the fact that there are others, the staff of the United Nations and some of the Diplomatic Corps, for whom it is a daily two-way passage.

Apart from Jerusalem, and Aqaba which is practically cheek by jowl with Eilat, few tourists visit the other frontier towns and villages for they have little to offer in the way of archaeological and Biblical sites and in any case are mostly under some kind of military restriction because of their position.

Most of the two hundred thousand or so people who live in these off-the-beaten-tourist track villages and small towns are farmers, as their families have been for countless generations. But many of them were left with no land to till nor orchards and vineyards to cultivate when the armistice line was drawn up in 1949. Some villages were even cut off from their churches, mosques, schools and freshwater springs. Those families who still had their own roofs over their heads could not be classified as refugees and so obtain UNWRA relief, even though they might have been left destitute, as many were.

143

Arab farmers could watch the new Jewish settlers ploughing the land and gathering the harvests that had been theirs. No wonder that they sometimes stole across the line at night to take the oranges, peaches and olives that they considered were still their own, or to visit relatives and friends who had not been able to leave once the cruel division was made.

These little excursions sometimes ended in bloodshed for the intruders ran the risk of being shot at by the Jewish Army patrols and there was always the added danger that the Israelis might claim the intrusion was an 'aggressive' violation of the armistice line and retaliate, endangering women and children. If the Arabs were caught crossing the line by their own police or soldiers, they were arrested and imprisoned, for from the start Jordan has done her best to prevent border incidents and infiltration from both sides.

But until Jordan's frontier patrol could be effectively built up this two-way watch was an almost superhuman task. One could buy real Jaffa oranges in the streets of Amman and Jerusalem for the first few years after the war, at practically give away prices. 'Oranges brought straight from Jaffa by our own infiltrators,' the vendors used to cheekily cry, seeing nothing wrong with slipping over the line at harvest time to collect what they felt was their rightful own. The price of oranges went up sharply when this kind of trading was stamped out by Jordan's police and Army.

It is due to their constant vigilance and the help of sharp-eyed Bedouin along the remote southern stretch of the armistice line that there are not more two-way violations of the frontier; incursions by frustrated Palestinian refugees who still remember every street, tree and stone of the towns, villages and farms they had to leave behind, and savage 'reprisal' raids into Jordan by Israeli commandos.

The first time I visited one of the frontier villages was by invitation to meet the *mukhtar,* the headman, of Beit Safafa, a little farming community in the hills near Bethlehem where a high fence of barbed wire – the line – runs straight down the middle of the main street dividing one side to the Arabs, the other to the

Jews. Children, some of them cousins, for a few Arab families had stayed behind during the shooting war to keep a claim on their property, were coming out of schools on both sides of the wire. They passed within touching distance – they daren't touch one another through the wire – without speaking or smiling to those on the other side.

As I was standing in this divided street an armoured patrol car filled with young Israeli soldiers, steel-helmeted, cradling machine guns in their arms and one of them with a walkie-talkie radio, drove slowly down the other side of the fence. 'They have come to see who you are. They keep a constant watch from that house over there on everyone new who goes near the wire,' said one of the villagers who was standing with me.

The Jewish soldiers smiled as they saw me put away my camera and heard us talk in English, but I felt it was the smile on the face of the tiger. Soon after I was sitting under a fig tree having a cup of tea with the *mukhtar* and some of the villagers, and he was explaining that the big new apartment blocks we could see on the other side had been built for Jewish immigrants 'with American money' and that the Israeli train chugging in from Lydda on the Mediterranean coast about forty miles away had been provided 'by the British and the Germans'. For a moment there was bitterness in his face and voice, but he remembered I was his guest and traditional Arab hospitality and good nature won. Soon we all were laughing and smiling again and talking about other things.

The next time I went to the frontier it was at my own urgent request. I had work to do. News had just come through of a three-point Israeli attack in the north, the biggest for eight years, and I had to cable a report.

From a reporter's point of view, I had a 'scoop' although it was an unhappy one. That evening I was at a dinner party in Zerka, about twelve miles north of Amman, when suddenly my host, a high-ranking Army officer, was called to the telephone. He came back into the dining room looking grave and after a short consultation with another officer, who was also a guest, told the rest of us that unfortunately they would have to leave at once since they had just been given news of a frontier attack that sounded serious. Within minutes, the host had changed into uniform and left for Amman where King Hussein had called an emergency military meeting.

I shot back to Amman too, and, after getting military permission to go up to the places that had been attacked, arrived soon after dawn at Jenin, a farming town and market centre on the armistice line north of Nablus and on the old, pre-armistice road to Haifa which lies about thirty miles away. There is a local tradition that Jenin was the 'certain town' in Samaria in which Christ cured the ten lepers, one of whom, the only one to return and thank Him, was a Samaritan and to whom Christ then said, '. . . thy faith hath made thee whole'.

There was a throng of people in the main street staring at what was left of three buildings, a cornmill, an icemaking plant and a shop. All three had been blown up. The Governor of the district, Hamdi Khalaf, arrived and told me that as far as they knew from reports still being pieced together, two large groups of Israeli commandos had entered the town just before midnight. One had branched off to the outskirts of the town to dynamite these buildings. The other group had covered their dynamiting party's advance and tried to divert attention by firing at buildings in the centre of the town.

The first group had been surprised on their way back before the explosions and firing started, by a frontier patrol of Jordanian soldiers. There was a short exchange of fire and two Jordanians were wounded. 'From the tracks we have found the Jews must have entered the town through those orange groves,' the Governor said, pointing to the thickly planted orchards surrounding one side of the town and extending to no man's land. 'They took advantage of the darkness for there was no moon last night.'

A young policeman drew a map in the dusty street for me, showing how the Israelis must have come in. 'They claim that we attacked Affoulah, which is just over the frontier not far from here, a few days ago, but I know we didn't,' he said, almost choking with grief and anger.

The Governor took me to see the other point of attack. A small Latin church and an adjoining block of offices and shops were peppered with what looked like machine-gun fire. A priest was standing outside the church examining bullet holes in the door. He had just picked up one spent bullet that had gone through the heavy door, across the church porch and out into a garden twenty yards beyond. Outside one of the shops the owner, a shoe-maker, was displaying to a large group of onlookers a handful of bullets he had found inside his workshop. The shutters of his win-dow were as full of holes as a sieve. The remains of nineteen mor-tar bombs fired in this part of the town had been collected by the Army and placed in a pile of sand in the street. A ring of curious small boys and men were gathered round the ugly-looking heap.

'The King has just left,' the Governor said. 'He was here in-specting the scenes of the attacks and went to see the two soldiers who are now in hospital. One of them is seriously wounded in the stomach and the King has sent for a blood transfusion from Am-man.' The badly wounded boy was still unconscious when I saw him, but the other soldier was propped up in bed and was being visited by friends. He had been wounded in both legs and had been congratulated by the King on being safe. 'I told Hussein that we shall fight to the last man and the last bullet,' this young soldier told me. He was a Palestinian, born in Haifa, and could not have been more than twenty years old.

King Hussein had just arrived in Amman after driving himself up the two hundred and nine miles from Aqaba that evening, when news of the attack came through. He had attended the meeting at military headquarters, then insisted on driving himself up to the frontier. He is an expert fast driver and knew he could get himself there more quickly than anyone else would care to drive him. On the way back to Amman, weariness obviously over-came him. He must have dozed at the wheel for he drove into a wall, hurting his back, an injury for which he later had to have treatment. But in spite of all this he was at the airport in Amman at noon to meet the Vice-President of India who was visiting Jordan.

Qualqilya, south of Jenin and not far from Nablus, is a military area since it is in a pocket that bulges into the armistice line. It is also a farming community, and during that night one of its schools and a petrol station had been dynamited by Israeli infiltrators. By the time I got there the petrol store was a smouldering, black ruin and what had been a school was full of bewildered boys examining classrooms blown open to the sky and desks covered with debris and broken glass. Again it seems the infiltrators had crept into the town through surrounding orchards and by their tracks there must have been about fifty of them.

The third place that had been attacked that night was Shuneh, a village in the north near the Syrian border. All three attacks had been simultaneous. It was a carefully planned military operation.

Back in Jerusalem, emergency headquarters had been set up in one of the hotels and I met one of Jordan's Ministers there who told me that already the Israelis were claiming over the radio that their three-pronged attack had been a reprisal for three incidents they claimed had taken place on their side of the truce line a few days before. The Minister said that before this 'reprisal' Jordan had already been exonerated of two of these incidents by United Nations investigators and the third, at Affoulah, was still under study. I had noticed the distinctively white-painted United Nations cars were already at the frontier where I had been. Their crews of observers were wasting no time in investigating this latest trouble and collecting evidence which would be sifted rapidly and carefully by the UN Truce Supervision Organisation in Jerusalem.

In the past, reports of the Organisation had clearly shown up the vital difference between the many incidents that had happened on both sides of the truce line. Arabs who crossed in breach of the armistice, whether Jordanians or others, had been found to be acting independently, in defiance of the Government of Jordan. More than once Jordan had been given credit by the UN Truce Supervision Organisation for doing all she could to help keep the frontier calm and prevent infiltration from her side by arresting and imprisoning offenders. But Israeli infiltration had almost always been shown to be military attacks, carefully planned and carried out, instead of prevented, by Israeli forces, as the three had been that night.

Soon afterwards, newspapers in Beirut were carrying reports of claims made by an organisation calling itself El Fateh, an elusive underground 'Palestine Liberation Movement' of saboteurs which Israel maintains is trained in Syria and has many Palestinian refugees in its band. El Fateh's claims were that it alone had been responsible for the recent assaults on Israel, the assaults for which Israel had lashed out at Jordan. How and from which Arab country El Fateh slips into Israel or whether it is a secret force actually working from inside is known only to El Fateh. Jordan emphatically disclaims this organisation which adds to her burden of vigilance and which certainly seems to be aggravating rather than helping her already heavy responsibilities on the armistice line.

But the Israeli Foreign Minister was reported to have said on this occasion that it was not Israel's duty to check who is responsible for El Fateh attacks and that the only important thing as far as they were concerned was over which Arab border they had come – Jordan, Lebanon, Syria or Egypt.

Once again tension in the Middle East was stretched very close to snapping point. But once again it gradually relaxed, after quivering dangerously, and shrank back to its usual extent.

Hebron, City of Abraham

THE CLATTER OF a string of blue glass beads against the dash-board or windscreen is something all taxis from Cairo to Damascus have in common. Donkeys and camels all over the Middle East have their lucky blue beads too. So have the babies and small children. The girls wear them as earrings or bracelets, the boys have them sewn on to their felt caps.

Blue is the lucky colour in the Middle East and is supposed to ward off the evil eye. So instead of touching wood, or throwing a pinch of salt over their shoulders, the Arab villagers paint their door frames blue, and buy blue beads. And the luckiest blue beads of all come from Hebron where they are blown from drops of molten glass by four men sitting round an open furnace in a cave-like workshop.

But beads are not the only things they make, although one would think so from the numbers that are exported all over the Moslem world. It is fascinating to watch these glass-blowers blow and twirl the glowing drops of red-hot glass at the end of their long blowing tubes and wonder what they are going to produce next. It might be a slender-necked jug or vase, exactly like the Roman ones you can see in the Palestine Museum in Jerusalem, a bowl, plate, jar or a fat candlestick that tilts crazily to one side as it hardens so that it will always look as if it is melting.

A deep Mediterranean blue is the traditional colour of Hebron glass, but sometimes the molten glow at the end of the tube cools down to green, amethyst, topaz or amber, depending on the formula the glass-blowers have used when mixing their ingredients. These formulae are the closely guarded secrets of one family in Hebron, and have been so from the time when the art of glass blowing first came to this ancient town in Palestine, from Phoenicia.

Modern chemical formulae might be used today instead of the old ones that included the natural minerals found in the sandy soil around Hebron and modern shapes might be produced, tumblers, ashtrays and lamp bases, to please the tourists and to furnish the new hotels in Jordan. But the men sitting cross-legged round the furnace work in exactly the same way as did the Phoenicians, the people who discovered how to make glass and took the art to Egypt and Rome. The famous Venetian glass works on the island of Murano are direct descendants of the first Phoenician workshops, but it is in Hebron where you can watch glass being made in a way that the old Phoenician craftsmen would recognise at once.

Some of the oldest examples left of Hebron glass date back to the time of the Crusades and are in two windows in Hebron's Haram Al-Ibrahimi As-Sheriff Mosque, which is built over the tombs of Abraham, his son Isaac, grandson Jacob and their wives, Sarah, Rebecca and Leah. 'See how soft the colours are, how they glow like jewels,' said the Sheik of the Mosque as he pointed the windows out to me. The sun shining through the glass made pools of glorious colour on the marble and mosaic lined interior. 'The formulae used by the ancient glass makers were not the same as those used today,' the Sheik said. 'The old ones have been forgotten and other ingredients have taken their place, so that although the modern colours might be copies, they are harsher.'

Windows like those in the mosques of Palestine might well have been the inspiration of the tradition of stained glass windows in our own churches brought back to Europe by the Crusaders, as they brought back ideas for architecture, embroidery and furnishings.

Hebron is one of the oldest constantly inhabited towns in the world and was built, according to the Bible, seven years before Tanis (Zoan), the chief town in Lower Egypt. It was David's capital for seven and a half years until he captured Jerusalem. He was crowned King there, and the first six of his sons, including his favourite, Absolom, were born there. Later Absolom made it the headquarters of his tragic revolt against his father.

The Arab name for Hebron is Khalil Ar-Rahaman, the City of the Friend, for Abraham, who is venerated by Islam as the Friend of God and the First Moslem, lived here. The story of how he was visited by the three angels as he sat in his tent door in the heat of the day on the plains of Mamre, just outside Hebron, and how he bought the nearby cave of Machpelah as a tomb for his wife Sarah, where later he, Isaac, Jacob and their wives were also buried, is told in Genesis. Hebron is visited by many of the Moslem pilgrims who travel by road through Jordan to Mecca so that they can pray at the tomb of Abraham, one of the holiest places in the Moslem world.

The cave of Machpelah is beneath Hebron's As-Sheriff Mosque and is inaccessible. Even the guardians of the Mosque have been forbidden to enter it for centuries. The Crusaders who called the Haram area and its buildings the Castle of St Abraham and turned the place into garrison quarters, a church and a monastery, opened the cave in the twelfth century and examined the tombs of the Patriarchs before clamping down the flagstones and sealing it up.

Cenotaphs draped with moss green silk tapestries, richly embroidered with gold thread, stand over the cave and are believed to mark the exact burial places. The only direct opening to the cave is a hole in the floor of the Mosque from which a lighted oil lamp is suspended, but little can be seen of what lies below.

Leah, the first of Jacob's wives, was 'tender-eyed', but Rachel, her younger sister, was 'beautiful and well favoured' and it was for Rachel that Jacob willingly served the sisters' father for fourteen years. But Rachel is not with her husband in Hebron. She is buried on the road to Bethlehem, where she died giving birth to Benjamin.

The grapes that grow in the vineyards around Hebron are as famous today as they were in Biblical times when Moses sent

152

men to spy out the land of Canaan, in which Hebron stood. The spies came back with pomegranates and figs and a bunch of grapes so enormous that two of them had to carry it between them on a staff. This was the land flowing with milk and honey, and it still is. But there is an even older tradition in Hebron that this was also the place where the first vine was planted after the flood by Noah.

During the Crusades, Hebron was a Frankish garrison controlling the Negeb desert, and it was from this town that Baldwin set out with a tiny army of about six hundred men and crossed the burning Sinai peninsular to campaign against Egypt. He reached the Nile but fell sick and was carried back to Palestine, where he died, and was buried in the Church of the Holy Sepulchre in Jerusalem. Saladin recaptured Hebron from the Crusaders and the As-Sheriff Mosque was eventually rebuilt by the Moslem leader who followed him, Bibars.

But in spite of its great antiquity, Hebron has been largely ignored, until recently, by archaeologists, although some now feel that this might be one of the most promising places for excavation in Jordan. Test digs so far have uncovered buildings dating from medieval Islam and Roman times – the great enclosing walls of the Haram, the sacred area round the Mosque, are largely Herodian – and have laid bare much older defence walls, built on bed rock.

Reports that the archaeologists now digging in Hebron planned to explore the burial sites of the Patriarchs caused dismay among Orthodox Jewry in America, but were denied by King Hussein when he visited the United States in 1964 for the opening of the Jordan Pavilion at the New York World's Fair. The King said that the graves of Abraham and his family, which are equally sacred to Christians and Moslems as well as Jews, would not be included in the excavations.

So the flagstones replaced by the Crusaders eight hundred years ago are not to be disturbed again. But the layers of history lying beneath the gardens, orchards, streets and souks of modern Hebron will be a happy hunting ground for the archaeologists and might throw a new light on the lives of the Patriarchs and the days recorded in Genesis.

Hebron was a front line town in the fighting between Arab and Jew in the Palestine war, lying as it does on the important road from Jerusalem through the Negeb desert to Beersheba and Gaza. Close to Hebron, on the road to Bethlehem, was the Jewish settlement of Kafr Etzion from which many ambushes were directed against the Arab convoys using the road. This settlement was the first occupied by the Jordanian Army during the fighting as a move to keep the road to Hebron open, and it is now one of Jordan's frontier villages. It is a peaceful enough looking place, of farmlands and orchards, but faces a formidable stretch of armistice line.

It was typical of King Hussein to choose this place for presenting colours to some of the first brigades of the National Guard to be amalgamated into the Jordanian Army. On a wide grassy slope, under what must have been the very watchful eyes of the Jewish demarcation line guards, a platform was built from which Hussein could review his troops, and rows of chairs set out for guests who were invited to watch the parade.

It is always a thrill to hear Hussein's soldiers roar out a welcome to their King, and on that morning, Jordan's Independence Day and the fourth anniversary of the King's marriage to Muna al Hussein, they made the hills around Kafr Etzion ring. He acknowledged their enthusiasm by shaking hands with every one of them after the parade.

Jordan, like other Arab countries, had just severed its diplomatic relations with West Germany because of the support Germany had decided to give to the Israelis, and in his speech to his soldiers Hussein reminded them of 'the most recent aggressive aims of the Zionists – an attack on Arab rights to the waters of the River Jordan and a plan to use them to irrigate the Negeb desert and prepare it for large scale Israeli immigration'. This, he said, would threaten the security of the area and with it, the security of the whole world.

It was late May and the Jordan was beginning to flow less

rapidly as the winter rains dried up. Tension was higher in the Middle East than it had been since the use of the waters first came into dispute. The Israelis had plans to pump large supplies of water out of Lake Tiberius (the Sea of Galilee) and store it in a reservoir before carrying it two hundred miles south, by pipeline and canal, to the Negeb.

The Arabs had counter plans for preventing what they feared would be an increase of salinity in the River Jordan and a flow reduced to a mere trickle as the Israelis pumped supplies out of Lake Tiberius.

The headwaters of the Jordan are three rivers, the Baniyas and the Dan, springing from the slopes of Mount Hermon in Syria, and the Hasbani, which starts in Lebanon. These tributaries unite in the Upper Jordan which flows into Lake Huleh and Lake Tiberius before being joined by the Yarmuk, the Jordan's main tributary. The Yarmuk also rises in Syria and meets the Jordan at what is often a skirmishing ground for Arab and Jewish forces, just south of Lake Tiberius, near the point where the borders of Syria, Jordan and 'Israel' meet. From then on the River Jordan flows through the Jordan Valley to empty into the Dead Sea.

Jordan believes that the Israeli pumping operations at Lake Tiberius will dry up thousands of acres of farmland in the northern part of the kingdom and deprive fifty thousand people of their only means of livelihood. The Lake Tiberius scheme could also mean that Jordan's plans to turn large areas of arid ground in the Jordan Valley into more farmland would have to be abandoned, and this land is urgently needed.

I had to cross the Jordan on my way to Amman after the parade, and still thinking of what Hussein had said about the security of the whole world, I stopped when I reached the river and walked down the steep bank near the place where John is thought to have baptised Christ and where last year the Pope stood and blessed the enormous crowd that had gathered around him.

Soldiers of the Jordanian Army, guarding the bridge that crosses the river at this point, were scanning the road for signs of the King's car, for he was going to Amman, as well, to join his

155

family for a wedding anniversary celebration. A Bedouin boy drove a flock of fat-tailed sheep through the tamarisks that skirt the road, and in the distance the purple and brown mountains of Moab rose above the deceptively blue Dead Sea to which the river was hurrying and in which it too would die. All rivers run into a salt sea somewhere and this one is no different. But what the Jordan does before its end is more significant than the course of any other river.

The Jordan gave life to early man in Palestine and hope to the early Christians. Now once again it is a river of destiny for mankind. World peace might well depend on the way its life giving waters are used by Arab and Jew, this year, next year, or the year after.

Travel Intelligence

FOOD

Good trenchermen are appreciated in Jordan, where there is an Arab proverb that the amount of food a guest eats equals his affection for his host. Arab food is something of an adventure, but a delicious one. It is a fascinating amalgamation of culinary ideas brought to this part of the world by all the nations who some time or other have settled here; from the Romans, who had a passion for using herbs and honey, to the Turks whose gourmet dishes make them the great classical cooks of the Middle East.

It is a tradition of Arab hospitality that only the best is good enough for a guest, and the best Arab food takes plenty of preparation. It is not something that can be whipped up in minutes and brought to the table by the time the guest has had a welcoming cup of coffee or an aperitif. This is one of the reasons why the best Arab food is found in speciality restaurants, apart from in private homes where cooking is still a traditional art.

The kitchen staff in most of the hotels that cater for tourists have not the time to spend on making elaborate Arab dishes and perhaps in any case have been discouraged by those who will not venture into the unknown, and always ask for 'Continental' food. Some of these hotels tempt their guests with the more familiar looking local dishes, *kebab*, grilled pigeon and *baclawa*, the Turkish sweet that has become popular in coffee bars and delicatessens all over the world. Sometimes they will tempt a little further with *mensaf*, the national dish of Jordan, *mousakhan*, a famous Palestinian dish of chicken, and an *hors-d'œuvre* of highly seasoned pastes and pickles to be eaten with flat Arab bread.

157

But for a real taste of Jordan's cookery, look for those little places that are crowded at lunchtime with local businessmen and ask any one of them, or the proprietor who will be hovering between the kitchen and the tables, to help you with the menu if it is only written in Arabic.

You will probably be invited to start off with *mezzeh,* an *hors-d'œuvre* selection that can be a meal in itself. The table will be spread with nuts, olives and strips of raw and pickled vegetables – watch out for the little hot peppers unless you have an asbestos-lined mouth. Dip pieces of the large round of flat Arab bread that will be served with your *mezzeh* into the dishes containing *hummus, tabouli* and *batinjaan bi taheeni* pastes and *lebne,* which is a soft, white goat's milk cheese not to be confused with *laban,* which is yoghourt and is sometimes served alone or mixed with chopped mint and cucumber.

Hummus is a thick, smooth paste made from a purée of chick-peas mixed with lemon juice and sesame oil (*taheeni*) and flavoured with garlic. *Tabouli* is a finely chopped salad made from cracked wheat (*burghul*), mint, parsley, onions, tomatoes, oil and lemon juice. *Batinjaan bi taheeni,* or *mutabal,* is a rougher textured paste than *hummus* and is made from the flesh of baked eggplants mashed with lemon juice and *taheeni* and flavoured with garlic. *Arak,* a white spirit made at its best from grapes, is the local aperitif to drink with your *mezzeh.* Sometimes *arak* is made from figs or dates when it is stronger, cheaper, but not so good for you. Better leave this to those who are used to it.

For the main dish there will be a choice of chicken, pigeon, lamb or mutton, cooked in a variety of ways. The most popular way of cooking chicken in Jordan provides a very filling dish called *mousakhan,* the pride of Ramallah, a resort town just north of Jerusalem. The first time I ate this I tried to break down the ingredients in the hope of being able to serve it as a supper party dish at home, but was completely thrown by the main flavouring which I thought was fresh lemon juice but which came from a bright red berry called *summak* which was finely ground and thickly spread over the whole thing. A whole chicken is split open, placed on a

158

round of flat Arab bread, smothered with onions that have been lightly fried in oil, sprinkled liberally with *summak*, then grilled under a charcoal fire. The oil and chicken juices soak into the bread and help to crispen the exposed edges, which should not be overlooked when eating this delicious dish.

Lamb and mutton will be served in so many different ways that most of the time you will have to ask what the dish is. It will be most difficult to identify. *Kebab* is easy enough, just cubes of tender lamb that might or might not have been marinaded and sprinkled with herbs before being grilled on a skewer. But *kibbeh, shawarma, koftah* (or *kafta*), *fatteh* and *mensaf* need explaining.

Kibbeh is lamb pounded to a paste with cracked wheat and onions. Sometimes it is served raw, like steak tartar, or it is pressed into a large, flat tray, sprinkled with fried, chopped pine nuts and then baked, to be served hot or cold. Another way is to mould it into little cakes, like hamburgers, and grill them.

Shawarma is a cone of slices of highly seasoned lamb, cooked on a slowly revolving spit in front of a charcoal fire. As the meat cooks, slices are cut off, usually to be served with *hummus*. You can see this dish being cooked on the pavement outside some of the smaller Arab restaurants in the souks, and the appetising smell, drifting down the street, draws hungry men like bees to a honeypot.

Koftah is seasoned, ground lamb, sometimes baked in a tray or grilled as little cakes, like *kibbeh,* or moulded into sausage shapes and grilled over charcoal on a skewer. Like *kebab, koftah* is usually served with salad.

Fatteh is rather more of an acquired taste than the previous ways of serving lamb or mutton, and is a traditional winter dish. It is made from pieces of spiced, preserved mutton, cooked in a broth to which yoghourt, melted butter, pine nuts, garlic and mint are added and, sometimes, toasted bread.

Mensaf is the national dish of Jordan, the one you will be served if you are fortunate enough to be entertained by the Bedouin in their black tents. At its desert simplest it is boiled lamb or mutton, served on top of a huge mound of rice and covered with the piping hot gravy in which the meat has been cooked. When it is more elaborate the sauce is thickened with yoghourt, finely chopped onions and melted butter and the meat is garnished with fried pine nuts.

The Arabs cook vegetables with imagination and care and never seem to boil them to a watery death. The *mahshi,* the stuffed vegetables, are almost a meal in themselves and take time to prepare. These can be marrow, squash and eggplant, the flesh scooped out and mixed with chopped meat, rice and nuts, then stuffed back into the shell. Cabbage, peppers and vine leaves are also stuffed this way.

The most popular Arab sweetmeat in Jordan is *knafeh* which is quite unlike anything I have ever tasted before and is a mixture of sweet and savoury tastes. It is made from melted white cheese topped with *vermicelli* cooked in butter and sugar syrup, the whole sprinkled with chopped *pistachio* nuts, then baked in a large tray.

Sweetmeat making is usually the job of the specialised pastry-cook shops, so few restaurants bother to make their own. A familiar sight in the streets before lunchtime is the delivery boys, carrying large trays of *knafeh,* little doughnuts, sweet batter fritters soaked in syrup, and *baclawa,* which is made from layers of paper thin, crisp pastry, stuffed with chopped nuts and sugar and covered with honey or syrup while still hot from the oven.

SHOPPING

Gold is the souvenir that takes my spending money in Jordan. It is cheaper there than I have found it anywhere else and is sold by the weight, often without much financial account being taken of the fine handwork which has gone into making a piece of jewellery. It is usually twenty or twenty-two carat and although not hallmarked, is the genuine stuff, if you are careful to buy from a reputable goldsmith. Your hotel or the Tourist Office will be able to recommend one.

For a few pounds there is an enormous choice of gold rings set with semi-precious stones such as topaz, turquoise, cornelian and amethyst, five-banded 'harem' rings studded with jewels that can be real or fake, depending on how much you want to spend, and for a little more, you might, if you are lucky, come across a matching 'harem' bracelet. They are not as easily found as the 'harem' rings since in spite of their name they are rather Victorian in character and are not designed to wear with today's casual fashions.

Silver is cheaper in Jordan than in other places too and is fashioned into coffee spoons, boxes, little bowls and other *bric-à-brac* for the home, as well as jewellery.

The jeweller's shop is by no means the only place in which to find fine handwork. Olive wood, with its distinctive graining of whorls and wavy lines that are dark brown against a warm honey colour, is carved into boxes, bowls, rosaries and tableaux of the Nativity, the Three Kings, camel caravans and village life. To any collector of treen these small carvings are a delight to handle and look at, for in the best pieces the grain is always used to highlight the curve of a face, the neck of a camel, the flow of a Bedouin robe in the way that a painter uses brush strokes.

Sometimes the olive wood boxes are inlaid with a mosaic of mother-of-pearl. The oldest centre of the mother-of-pearl carving craft is in Bethlehem where you can see for yourself how many hours of intricate work go into making one inlaid box or the carved covers for a Bible or missal. The mother-of-pearl is carved into elaborate filigree jewellery too; earrings, brooches and pendants shaped like Crusader crosses, stars, flowers and arabesque patterns.

Pottery that is handpainted in the patterns and colours of an oriental carpet is a distinctive sign that it comes from the Palestine Pottery in Jerusalem. For a few shillings you can buy coffee cups, mug, plates, tiles, bowls, ashtrays, doorknobs, jugs and tea and coffee pots beautifully painted with stylised flowers, birds and desert gazelles against rich backgrounds of blue, brown, terracotta, or plain white. If you cannot find what you want the pottery will make it for you. For years I had been looking for a large, covered bowl in which I could keep the *pot-pourri* I make every summer. The lid of the bowl had to be pierced so that the scent of the dried petals and herbs could percolate through without being quickly dispered, as it is if the mixture is kept in an open bowl. The pottery had almost the right thing, a deep, covered bowl, decorated with flowers and a peacock in a tree, but there were no holes in the lid. I explained what I wanted, and they made it for me exactly, and cleverly placed the holes in the centre of the flowers so that they looked like part of the pattern. My *pot-pourri* bowl has now become part of the range that is regularly kept in stock.

One of the oldest crafts in the Holy Land is embroidery and the women of Bethlehem and Ramallah and the smaller villages and Bedouin tribes still use it to decorate the bodice, sleeves and skirt of their flowing gowns. Each district has its own pattern of stitches and there are three traditional forms. The oldest is Byzantine in origin, intricate geometrical patterns of cross-stitch usually worked in black and red thread. The Persian influence shows stylised leaves, flowers and fruit worked in satin stitch and brilliant colours. The Crusaders left behind their medieval preference for richly decorating velvet, wool and silk with gold and silver thread and this kind of embroidery is still the speciality of Bethlehem. The Persian and Crusader methods of embroidery are mostly used for collector's pieces, but the Byzantine cross-stitch is more adaptable and looks attractive on modern table linen and cushion covers.

Hebron glass is cheap and unusual and the glass-blowers have started to make modern, practical things such as lamp-bases, beer mugs and lemonade sets in glowing green, amber and amethyst colours as well as in the traditional blue. From Hebron too come fleece-lined jackets, coats and slippers.

Antiques ranging from Roman clay lamps, ancient coins and Byzantine ikons to heavy pieces of Bedouin heirloom jewellery can be bought, mainly in Jerusalem. Sometimes objects found on archaeological sites that are surplus to the requirements of the Department of Archaeology can be bought from the museums in Jerusalem and Amman.

Objects of piety, such as crosses, rosaries, medals, Bibles, missals and figurines can, if they are made of 'solid material', be blessed by the Franciscan Fathers at the Latin Sacristy in the Church of the Holy Sepulchre. The Fathers will give you a certificate to show that the objects have been blessed, but point out that the indulgences acquired will be lost if the souvenirs are later sold.

Everywhere you go in Jordan you will be surrounded by Arabic music, on taxi radios, in the hotels, cafés and restaurants. Folk songs are popular and once you accept the fact that rhythm is more important than melody in this music, you will begin to appreciate it and might want to take home some records of it. These can be bought in Jerusalem and Amman.

The traditional Jordanian folk song is the *al hejeini* which is set to the rhythm of the camel's stride and is a very ancient form of music. Traditional instruments used by the musicians are reed flutes, the Bedouin *rabab*, which is a square-shaped, one-string violin; the *aud*, a pear-shaped kind of mandolin; the *ganoun*, an oriental harp; the tambourine *daff* or *riqq*; and the *durbukka*, an elongated clay drum stretched with skin. The *debkeh* is the national dance of the men and involves a great deal of gliding, stamping and rhythmic handclapping. It is more exciting to watch than listen to, but it also can be bought on records.

WHEN TO GO

April and May are perhaps the loveliest months in Jordan. The land is freshly green after the winter rains and the wild flowers are at their best. But even in the winter months of December, January and February and the early spring month of March, there will be sweetly scented polyanthus-narcissus, wild crocus, tulip, anemone, cyclamen and the green and white Star of Bethlehem in flower in the hills and valleys.

From June to October the sun toasts the land brown and only the hardy, heat-loving flowers like oleander and tamarisk thrive. But the cultivated gardens that can be watered every day and shaded where necessary by the careful planting of trees are full of roses, geraniums, lilies and lavender.

During winter, from the beginning of December to the middle of March, the weather is generally mild, but can be cold, par-

163

ticularly in Jerusalem which is two thousand five hundred feet above sea level and where snow sometimes falls, but rarely stays on the ground for more than seconds. This is the season for rain, but it usually only lasts for a day at a time and is followed by bright, sunny, but cool days. A warm topcoat, raincoat, light tweeds and sweaters should be packed for a winter holiday.

But if you are also going to the winter resorts of Aqaba on the Red Sea and Jericho and the Dead Sea in the Jordan Valley, take cottons, linens, silks and swimsuits. The winter temperatures in these places are often up in the eighties and during the summer are generally an uncomfortable hundred-plus.

Summers in Jordan are hot and dry, start at the beginning of June and go on until the end of September. But even on the hottest days the evenings are refreshingly cool, so it is wise to pack a light-weight coat, or sweater, for when the sun goes down.

The spring and autumn months of March, April, May, October and November are pleasantly warm and sunny during the day, but chilly at night. Cottons and light-weight suits can be worn most days, but coats and sweaters are needed too.

And whatever time of the year you go to Jordan, take comfortable walking shoes. In many places the ground is stony and hard going and you are bound to do quite a lot of walking.

GETTING AROUND
Good roads link all the important tourist places in Jordan and getting around is easy. The most usual way of travelling is to buy a seat in a taxi. These shared taxis run like buses at regularly scheduled times, are cheap, comfortable and one of the best ways of getting to know the Jordanians. Your fellow travellers will be just as anxious to point out all the interesting spots on the way and to tell you about themselves as they will be to find out all about you.

Fares of these and regular taxis are fixed, and the Tourist Office will give you a price list. The same office will also give you the fixed rate for self-drive and chauffeur-driven cars, and timetables of bus services and the Hejaz line train that comes from Damascus but at the moment only goes down as far as Ma'an. You can fly between Amman and Jerusalem and soon there will be regular flights down to Aqaba. There are plans for running air-conditioned Pullman buses on regular tours from Jerusalem and Amman to places of interest, including Petra.

Distances :

From Jerusalem to		From Amman to	
Bethlehem	11 miles	Jerash	30 miles
Hebron	27 miles	Madaba	21 miles
Jericho	22 miles	Kerak	74 miles
Nablus	40 miles	Petra	169 miles
Amman by the		Aqaba	209 miles
Salt road	66 miles	Azraq	69 miles
by the		Mushetta	24 miles
Dead Sea road	55 miles	Wadi Rumm	203 miles
Aqaba	210 miles	Jericho	40 miles
Petra	169 miles	Dead Sea	36 miles

Tourist Police in regular policeman's uniform but with a shoulder flash which distinguishes them are on duty at the airports in Jerusalem and Amman, and in the two cities. They are there to give you any assistance you might need.

There is also a new highway patrol operated by the Jordanian Police, covering the cities, towns and highways. The patrol cars are distinctively zebra-striped and the crews are trained to help motorists, handle accidents and give first aid attention when necessary.

ACCOMMODATION

Hotels in Jordan are inspected and classified by the Tourism Authority. At the moment there are only two de-luxe class hotels in the country, the Intercontinental on the Mount of Olives in Jerusalem and the Intercontinental Al Urdon (Jordan) in Amman. Rates in all the hotels are extremely reasonable, but since they vary slightly from year to year as they are re-assessed by the

165

Tourism Authority up-to-date price lists are best obtained from the Tourist offices. A ten-per-cent service charge is usually added to the rates, and for the busy Christmas and Easter periods hotels are allowed to increase their rates by twenty-five per cent.

The Jordan Government has recently built rest houses in some of the popular tourist places where facilities are scarce, and more are planned. The rest house at Petra has overnight accommodation as well as an excellent restaurant. The rest houses at Jerash, Hebron, Madaba, Ma'an and Ramtha on the Syrian border have toilet facilities and a restaurant. There is also a rest house with overnight accommodation on the Iraqi border at Station H4, for modern desert travellers. Similar facilities are also planned by Kerak and Ras El Negeb.

MONEY

This is easy enough to calculate if you are British, for the main unit is the Jordan Dinar which is equivalent to the pound Sterling. The dinar is divided into 1,000 fils. Ten fils are called a piastre and equal $2\frac{1}{2}$d; 350 fils equal one US dollar.

Fils	£ Sterling	US dollar	Swiss Francs	Italian Lira	Spanish Pesetos	German DM
1 Jordan Dinar (1,000 fils)	£1	2.80	12.50	1754	175	11.35
500 fils	10s	1.40	6.25	877	87.5	5.67
100	2s	0.28	1.25	175.4	17.5	1.13
50	1s	0.14	0.63	17.7	8.75	0.57
25	6d	0.07	0.31	43.9	4.4	0.28
10	$2\frac{1}{2}$d	0.03	0.12	17.54	1.75	0.11

The rate, as elsewhere, fluctuates slightly and sometimes a better rate can be obtained from the many authorised money changers in Jerusalem and Amman than from the hotels and banks.

USEFUL ADDRESSES
The most useful of all are the two main offices of the Jordan Tourism Authority, in Saladin Street, Jerusalem, near the offices of the Middle East Airlines, and in King Hussein Street, Amman, just below the offices of British Overseas Airways Corporation. In these offices you will be made extremely welcome and can obtain, without charge, a wide selection of maps and travel folders covering all the important holy and tourist places as well as hotel, taxi and car hire price lists. The Tourism Authority can also arrange for you to meet Jordanian families in their homes as part of its informal Visit the Jordan Family scheme.

POST AND CABLE OFFICES
There are Post Offices throughout Jordan in all cities and main villages. All are provided with full telegraphic and telephone services. A special centre for wireless telecommunication with Europe, America and Arab countries has been established recently at the Central Post and Telegraph Office, Wadi es Seer Street, Amman.

AIRLINES
International airline offices of Middle East Airlines, British Overseas Airways Corporation, Alitalia (Italian Airlines), Lufthansa (German), KLM (Dutch Airlines), Alia (Royal Jordanian Airlines), and Kuwait Airlines, are all in Saladin Street in Jerusalem, and in King Hussein Street in Amman. Saudi Arabian Airlines and Iraqi Airlines are in King Hussein Street, while United Arab Airlines have an office in Port Said Street, Jerusalem.

HEALTH
There are a number of excellent doctors in Jordan and, should you need it, a good hospital service. Your hotel will put you in touch with a doctor should it be necessary. Most modern drugs and all the internationally well-known cosmetic and toilet articles you

167

might need can be bought in the pharmacies, particularly in Jerusalem and Amman.

There are also many efficient travel and tourist agencies specialising in tours of the Holy Land. Your hotel or the Tourist office can given you lists.

CONSULATES IN JERUSALEM

Belgium (also acting on behalf of Luxembourg, Holland, and Austria), near Ambassador Hotel, Sheik Jarah Quarter.

France, Sheik Jarah Quarter.

Greece (also acting on behalf of Jugoslavia), near St Stephen's Gate, Old City.

Italy (also acting on behalf of Switzerland, Finland and Norway), Sheik Jarah Quarter.

Spain (also acting on behalf of Latin American countries, Portugal, Brazil, West Germany, Poland and Czechoslovakia), Sheik Jarah Quarter.

Sweden, near Government Hospital, Old City.

United Kingdom (also acting on behalf of Commonwealth countries, Ireland, Burma, Denmark and South Africa), Damascus Gate.

United States of America (also acting on behalf of Philippines, Japan, Korea), near YMCA, Nablus Road.

ENTERING JORDAN

Tourists will be granted a visa, valid for two journeys within a six months' period, at any Jordan port of entry on payment of one Jordanian dinar and the showing of a valid passport and a current certificate of smallpox innoculation. Visas can also be given of course by the Jordan Consulates abroad, before you leave.

By reciprocal agreement, US nationals are granted free visas.

Israelis are barred entry into Jordan and travel between Jordan and 'Israel' can only be one way. Tourists coming into Jordan via 'Israel' will be allowed to enter provided they have no Israeli visa in their passports. They must then leave Jordan direct or through neighbouring Arab countries. Re-entry into 'Israel' is not permitted. Tourists crossing into 'Israel' from Jordan must leave direct from that country, they cannot re-enter Jordan nor any of the neighbouring Arab countries.

CUSTOMS
You may take into Jordan duty-free personal effects, including radio, cameras, typewriter, fire-arms for hunting, two hundred cigarettes or twenty-five cigars or two hundred grammes of tobacco, one litre of wine or spirits. You may also take in one hundred Jordan Dinars in bank notes and any amount of foreign bank notes and travellers cheques. On leaving you may take out up to JD 100 and foreign bank notes and travellers cheques up to the amount declared on entry.

Jordan's Customs Officers are among the most courteous I have ever encountered, and should you need assistance the Tourist Police will be on hand to help you.

PHOTOGRAPHY
There is no ban on taking photographs in Jordan except in controlled military areas where you are unlikely to go anyhow. But if you want to photograph the Jordanians themselves, be polite enough to ask their permission first. You would expect it if the same were happening to you.

GETTING THERE
You can take your choice and go by air, train or car. Regular flights from Europe go direct to Amman by Alia, BOAC, Alitalia and KLM and from all the leading European capitals to Beirut from where you can catch a connection to Jerusalem and Amman, or drive overland via Damascus. From Beirut to Amman by car takes about eight hours, and if you do not want to hire one for yourself, you can buy a seat in one of the shared taxis that run to schedule.

The Hejaz railway connects Amman with Damascus in Syria, then Turkey and the European railways. A sea ferry service covering the short distance between Suez and Aqaba is being planned.

169

TO HELP YOU MAKE FRIENDS

The Jordanians will be delighted if you can manage even a few words of their language. The spellings I have used for the Arabic words are phonetical.

hello	*marhaba*
good morning	*sabah al-khayr*
how are you?	*keef al-haal?*
welcome	*ahlan wa sahlan*
goodbye	*khatrak*
if God wills	*insh'Allah*
I am well	*mabsoot*
thank you	*shookran*
please	*min fadlak*
I am sorry	*muta'assef*
yes	*naam* or *aywah*
no	*laa*
why?	*laish?*
what is your name?	*aysh ismak?*
maybe tomorrow	*yimkin bukra*
coffee	*gahwah*
tea	*shaie*
milk	*haleeb*
yoghourt (also milk, so be careful!)	*laban*
come on, go on	*yallah*
let's go	*imshi*
sugar	*sukkar*
how much?	*kam?*
airport	*matar*

170

Arabic Numerals

one	*wahad*
two	*ithnain*
three	*thalatha*
four	*arba'a*
five	*khamsah*
six	*sittah*
seven	*saba'a*
eight	*thamanyah*
nine	*tisa'ah*
ten	*asharah*

If you manage to get beyond the stage of armchair travelling and go to Jordan, as I hope you will, then *Al-yowm ahsan min bukra*, which means today is better than tomorrow, and *Assaalamu alaykum* – peace be with you.

Index

172